Travels with Figment

ON THE ROAD IN SEARCH OF Disney DREAMS

by Marty Sklar

Disney Legend and Imagineering Ambassador

Edited by **Leslie A. Sklar**
Preface by **Bob Weis**

DISNEP
EDITIONS
Los Angeles • New York

Also by Marty Sklar

Dream It! Do It!
My Half-Century Creating Disney's Magic Kingdoms

One Little Spark!
Mickey's Ten Commandments and
The Road to Imagineering

One Little Spark
Words and Music by Richard Sherman and Robert Sherman
© 1981 Wonderland Music Company, Inc. (BMI)
All Rights Reserved. Used With Permission.

Printed in the United States of America
First Hardcover Edition, November 2019

10 9 8 7 6 5 4 3 2 1

Library of Congress Cataloging-in-Publication Data
Names: Sklar, Marty, author. | Weis, Bob, writer of preface.
Title: Travels with Figment : on the road in search of Disney dreams / Marty
    Sklar; preface by Bob Weis.
Description: First hardcover edition. | Glendale, California : Disney
    Editions, an imprint of Disney Book Group, 2019.
Identifiers: LCCN 2019012120 | ISBN 9781368023122
Subjects: LCSH: Sklar, Marty. | Sklar, Marty--Anecdotes. | Imagineers
    (Group)--Employees--Biography. | Disney, Walt, 1901-1966--Friends and
    associates. | Disneyland (Calif.)--History. | Walt Disney World
    (Fla.)--History.
Classification: LCC GV1852.2.S55 S45 2019 | DDC 791.06/8--dc23

FAC-020093-19183

The Official Disney Fan Club
D23.com

For All of Marty's Families:

For the Sklar Family

Leah
Howard and Katriina
Gabriel and Hannah
Leslie
Rachel and Jacob

For the Imagineering Family

Imagineers
Past, Present, and Future

For the Family of Disney Fans Worldwide

The Magic has always been for you!

CONTENTS

PREFACE
by Bob Weis

When I think about "Mickey's Ten," I think of Marty and how deep his thinking was, yet how casual and understated he was on the surface. And I also think of how Mickey's Ten and Marty were so intertwined—like two trees that grew together over the years so completely that they can never be separated.

In fact, that also describes Marty's relationship with Walt Disney Imagineering. There is no way to unravel what's Marty's and what's Imagineering's in this bonded tree of imagination, innovation, and creativity we work to grow and keep healthy each day. And I am thankful for that.

The truth is the concise rigor of "the Ten" is invaluable, yet it also masks the fact that Marty had many more commandments—or, better stated, *advice* points for Imagineers to follow. (For those of you who knew Marty, you know that "advice" is a pretty soft word; you took

Marty's notes seriously, lest you receive a red-ink note card to remind you!)

I'll take the risky step of adding a few more commandments—seven to be exact—to Mickey's Ten, or Marty's Ten, as we should rightly call them. As the next generation of Imagineers uses them, we can do well to heed this additional advice I've gleaned over time from Marty, sometimes from notes written in red pen.

1. Respect talent and experience when people retire or leave for whatever reason; celebrate their achievements, and make sure future Imagineers learn from them.
2. The parks must change with the times! They're not fixed in time, and they're not museum pieces.
3. Ethics and creativity transcend company boundaries. All of us who live creative lives owe it to our communities to collaborate and contribute our talents for the better, locally and globally.
4. Diversity in background, gender, culture, age, and experience is our strength, a creative well we draw from. It is a small world, but a diverse and exciting one, too.
5. Trust collaboration. Individual contributions are priceless, but collaboration creates unexpected magic. A roomful of talented people can move mountains. Put them in there, lock the door, and just pass food under the door until they emerge with great ideas.
6. Walk the halls—an organization chart tells you nothing. People are everything, and they're out there interacting, discussing, and challenging each other in the halls every day. Go out and join the conversation.

7. This is a calling, not a job. To bring happiness, laughter, and fun to millions of people around the world is a joy, a privilege, and indeed a responsibility. Take your fun seriously, and know that creativity really matters. It matters more every day.

For his Ten, and for the many other commandments he articulated for us over the years, I thank Marty. Each day I do.

—Bob Weis
President, Walt Disney Imagineering

Note: You'll find the myriad ways Marty's Ten Commandments have affected our Imagineering family in Chapter 8, beginning on page 150.

A Word from the Sklars

This book is a testament to Marty Sklar's enduring legacy.

When Marty died, unexpectedly, on July 27, 2017, we in his family felt a jolt of shock and grief. None of us expected Marty to leave us so soon; with no warning or intimation that things were about to change, we had not braced ourselves for the shock. It soon became clear that the news of Marty's passing had also sent shock waves through his other "family," of Imagineers (past and present), colleagues in the themed entertainment business, collaborators in the corporate world, and admirers and Disney fans across the globe.

Just as we were unprepared for our loss, we were equally unprepared for the sympathy and fellowship that reverberated back to us. We were heartened and deeply moved by the wave of condolences that washed over us via phone calls, e-mails, cards, and charitable donations made in memory of Marty to Ryman Arts, the nonprofit arts education organization that he and Leah co-founded in 1990 with other Disney alumni to honor Herb Ryman, their friend and a great Disney illustrator.

Very soon after we lost Marty, and while condolences were still coming in, Imagineers began asking one pressing question: Would we publish Marty's third book, which he had nearly finished writing at the time of his death? The queries were coming from people Marty had mentored over the years, many of whom had been enlisted by him to contribute to this book. Marty had been so supportive of them, encouraging them in their work for Disney and, in many cases, their careers after they had left Imagineering, that they never hesitated to respond when Marty needed something. Their answer was always, "Yes!"

Responding to Marty's requests was their way of giving back, of honoring his faith in them, and of carrying on his legacy. Their contributions to this book would be their way of expressing their admiration for Marty and the impact he had on them—and would once again declare the value and importance of his seminal philosophy of creating successful themed entertainment, Mickey's Ten Commandments. And so, in those days after our collective shock, when we were asked if we were going to get Marty's book to the publisher, the answer, of course, was "Yes!"

Marty would normally have been actively involved in the editing, polishing, designing, and finishing-up process of getting this book to the presses. Rest assured that, although he wasn't with us to participate in those stages of the process, what we present to you here is *Marty's* book: his experiences, his stories, his perspective, and his voice.

This book is Marty's legacy—and his gift to *you*.

—Leslie A. Sklar

About This Book

I first met Marty Sklar in the mid-1980s when I was a young editor working for Steve Birnbaum, creating *Birnbaum's Walt Disney World—The Official Guide*. But it wasn't until 1995 that I had the chance to work closely with Marty and the Imagineers on several book projects. It was a wee bit intimidating, but at the same time the opportunity of a lifetime to learn from the master.

When Marty retired in 2009 he called to talk about doing his first book, which turned into *Dream It! Do It! My Half-Century Creating Disney's Magic Kingdoms*. To say that I was honored to be trusted with Marty's autobiography would be a great understatement.

Walt Disney knew what he was doing when he hired Marty, who was still a student at UCLA, in the mid-1950s. Marty had a gift for writing and would become Walt's main speechwriter. For me, Marty was the ultimate collaborator.

He welcomed guidance and editing, and our conversations about that first book and the second—*One Little Spark!*—were some of the most memorable of my career.

At the many events that we attended together to promote his books, I was inspired by the time Marty took with each and every fan, the kindness he showed to every reader, and the care he displayed in answering questions and giving advice. These moments were priceless lessons on leading and mentoring.

In July 2017, I had a chance to spend time with Marty at the D23 Expo. He updated me then on the progress he was making on his latest endeavor, *Travels with Figment*. But, sadly and shockingly, less than two weeks later, Marty passed away. It was—and remains—an enormous loss to so many people. Happily, his amazing legacy lives on. Luckily, Marty had finished the first draft of the book, and thanks to his wife, Leah, and daughter, Leslie, we can now bring *Travels with Figment* to you.

We've decided to leave the book essentially as he wrote it—a moment in time captured for posterity. We filled in a few blanks and we hope we've chosen the images Marty would have wanted for this new book.

So, dear reader, enjoy Marty's last book.

—Wendy Lefkon
Editorial Director, Disney Editions

INTRODUCTION:
A Word from Marty

So the Internet was supposed to make travel less necessary for conducting business? Well, of course it has—yet I still have several million-mile-plus airline certificates to prove the words of that Frank Sinatra song "Love and Marriage": "You can't have one without the other."

Now that I'm retired from The Walt Disney Company (since 2009, after fifty-four years, including thirty as the creative leader of Walt Disney Imagineering), I'm often asked to "tell more stories" about Walt Disney; about my experiences in meeting, working with, and "selling" ideas (including that Purple Dragon) to major industry figures in various fields; and, of course, about the Disney Parks and Resorts—and the Imagineers who created them. And I've got lots of stories; after all, I'm the only Disney cast member to participate in the opening of all twelve Disney parks around the world (probably a tribute to a young start, and a long life).

In February 2017, I was invited to be the featured speaker at the first Epcot International Festival of the Arts at Walt Disney World. The fans I met there reminded me, in question and answer sessions after my talks, how hungry they were for "inside stories" about the world of Disney. I had already told many stories about my experiences in two popular books published by Disney Editions: *Dream It! Do It! My Half-Century Creating Disney's Magic Kingdoms*, and *One Little Spark! Mickey's Ten Commandments and The Road to Imagineering*.

But that doesn't seem to be enough for the legion of Disney fans around the globe (*Dream It! Do It!* has also been published in Japanese, Mandarin, and Portuguese). That point was driven home to me by a fan who drove 125 miles from Jacksonville, Florida, to Orlando and told me, "When we heard last night that you were going to be here, we drove down this morning to meet you and get our books autographed!"

I should not have been surprised. When I spoke at Chicago's Museum of Science and Industry in 2014, the Kelley family told me that they drove all the way from Cleveland—six hours and 344 miles—so their teenager, Jacob, could meet me, ask questions, and get his books signed. (Jacob and I still correspond by e-mail.) And when I spoke at The Art of Disney store in Disney Springs at Walt Disney World, a couple in attendance from Lexington, Kentucky, informed me that they had driven all night—a distance of 832 miles—just to make sure they could say hello and get their books signed.

Wow! Twelve hours on the road! I don't pretend to be

some kind of rock star, but there is a definite cachet to being named a Disney Legend, an honor bestowed on me in 2001.

I really did not expect to write another book. But those Disney fans kept asking me whenever and wherever I spoke—from California to Florida and Chicago to Austin, Texas—for more. It was always: "When can we read and hear more stories about the Disney world you lived in for more than half a century?"—Walt's world, and beyond. So I've rummaged through my files, and searched my memories, to write a new book about my experiences.

My goal has been to tell new stories. In the following pages, you will meet fascinating people, go inside amazing places, and peek into secret worlds that I was privileged to visit.

About the Purple Dragon: We were so fortunate that Imagineers Steve Kirk and Tony Baxter created Figment and gave him the lead role in Epcot's original Journey into Imagination. Figment enticed Kodak to become a sponsor of a major Epcot pavilion—one of six in the Future World area at the grand opening on October 1, 1982. Figment really did spark our efforts; he gave Richard Sherman and Robert Sherman the inspiration for the words they wrote in a wonderful song called "One Little Spark." From then on, Figment was always a companion in spirit on our travels, because these words were always the key to our mission:

One bright idea
One right connection
Can give our lives
A new direction

So many times, we're stumbling in the dark
And then "Eureka!"
That little spark!

So hop aboard—Figment and I will try to make our travels interesting, fun, and full of good Disney stories.

CHAPTER 1

TRAVELS WITH WALT

The last forty-four years of my career at The Walt Disney Company were full of exciting challenges, Disney magic, and especially fun—the fun we had creating fun for millions of guests visiting Disney Parks and Resorts around the world.

But when I look back, it's hard to top my first ten years at Disney, when one of my assignments was to write personal material for Walt Disney himself. I must admit that when Walt died on December 15, 1966, it hit me harder than the day my father died several years later. I loved and respected my dad dearly; he was a wonderful role model. But I never had to think like Leon Sklar, the teacher and school principal. To ghostwrite for Walt Disney, thinking like Walt was essential. Dad passed away suddenly from a heart attack. We sensed a few weeks before Walt passed, however, that he was leaving us.

That did not make my task any easier the day Walt died. I was called to the office of E. Cardon Walker, then head of Disney marketing, placed in the office next to his, and given one hour to write the statement to be issued to the media and Disney employees in the name of Roy O. Disney, Walt's brother and chairman of the company. I'm very honored that on December 15, 2016, Disney CEO Bob Iger quoted from that message in a special ceremony marking the fiftieth anniversary of Walt's death. Iger later wrote me, "I have the whole piece you wrote, and what an amazing piece it is!"

December 15, 1966

TO: All Employees
FROM: Roy Disney

The death of Walt Disney is a loss to all the people of the world. In everything he did Walt had an intuitive way of reaching out and touching the hearts and minds of young and old alike. His entertainment was an international language. For more than forty years people have looked to Walt Disney for the finest quality in family entertainment.

There is no way to replace Walt Disney. He was an extraordinary man. Perhaps there will never be another like him. I know that we who worked at his side for all these years will always cherish the years and the minutes we spent in helping Walt Disney entertain the people of the world. The world will always be a better place because Walt Disney was its master showman.

As President and Chairman of the Board of Walt Disney Productions, I want to assure the public, our stockholders and each of our more than four thousand employees that we will continue to operate Walt Disney's company in the way that he has established and guided it. Walt Disney spent his entire life and almost every waking hour in the creative planning of motion pictures, Disneyland, television shows and all the other diversified activities that have carried his name through the years. Around him Walt Disney gathered the kind of creative people who understood his way of communicating with the public through entertainment. Walt's ways were always unique and he built a unique organization. A team of creative people that he was justifiably proud of.

I think Walt would have wanted me to repeat his words to describe the organization he built over the years. Last October when he accepted the "Showman of the World" award in New York, Walt said, "The Disney organization now has more than four thousand employees. Many have been with us for over thirty years. They take great pride in the organization which they helped to build. Only through the talent, labor and dedication of this staff could any Disney project get off the ground. We all think alike in the ultimate pattern."

Much of Walt Disney's energies had been directed to preparing for this day. It was Walt's wish that when the time came he would have built an organization with the creative talents to carry on as he had established and directed it through the years. Today this organization has been built and we will carry out this wish.

Walt Disney's preparation for the future has a solid,

creative foundation. All of the plans for the future that Walt had begun—new motion pictures, the expansion of Disneyland, television production and our Florida and Mineral King projects—will continue to move ahead. That is the way Walt wanted it to be.

Despite my frequent opportunities to write Walt Disney's various messages and statements—in Walt Disney Productions' annual reports to stockholders, Disneyland souvenir guides, the introduction of new projects in Florida and Disneyland (and a proposal for an all-year California resort at Mineral King), material for the 1964–65 New York World's Fair, presentations to major corporations, and the script for a film about his far-sighted concept for the community he called EPCOT (Experimental Prototype Community of Tomorrow)—I travelled with Walt on the company's Gulfstream One on only two occasions.

The first was a Burbank to New York flight as a "thank you" for our work on the New York World's Fair. Walt was so pleased with the company's accomplishments at the fair— four of the five most popular pavilions were created by the Imagineers—that he instituted a weekly cross-country trip and tour of the fair's highlights for dozens of those at Disney who had played a role in creating the four Disney shows.

My wife, Leah, and I had the honor of joining Walt and Lilly Disney on one of those trips. Our fellow passengers were director Ham Luske and art director Mac Stewart, plus their spouses. Ham and Mac were longtime colleagues in animation; among their achievements was the animated penguin sequence featured with the live-action dancing of Julie Andrews and Dick Van Dyke in *Mary Poppins*. They had also produced the "Disneyland Goes to the World's Fair" television episode of *Walt Disney's Wonderful World of Color*, and two years later turned my script for Walt's EPCOT film into a twenty-five-minute explanation and marketing piece trumpeting a future Walt Disney World.

Walt made us feel at home immediately on board the Gulfstream One. There were two separate compartments in the aircraft, each with its own bathroom. Walt and Mrs. Disney occupied the larger area in the rear, but Walt made sure, as he stood in the doorway between the compartments, that Mrs. Disney could not hear him when he told the ladies in our group, "You're welcome to use the bigger bathroom in the rear compartment—don't let Madame Queen intimidate you!"

Walt was enamored of that Gulfstream, and of a smaller Beechcraft King Air that he put in service in the 1960s as a daily commuter flight between Burbank and Anaheim. The King Air left Burbank at 10:00 a.m. and arrived in Orange County (Anaheim's locale) about 10:30, with transportation then provided from the airport to Disneyland. Then everything was reversed at 4:00 p.m. I lived in Anaheim at the time and tried several times to make the service work for me—after all, it was great having a cup of coffee while looking down on that long line of traffic on the Santa Ana Freeway. But for me as a daily regimen, it just did not work—it cut into my work hours. And in the days before cell phones, it was hard to explain to Walt why he could not reach you by phone for a good part of the day . . . even when it was his idea!

On those cross-country flights in the Gulfstream, Walt especially loved the refueling stop at Grand Island, Nebraska, where fields of summer corn and wheat stretched as far as the eye could see. As we approached our landing, we could see the bright red carpet the folks who ran the fueling station had rolled out minutes before our arrival. And for many of us, the refueling was not the prime reason for stopping there. That particular fuel station was 100 percent a family-owned business; the cakes and pies "Mom" made were much more of an attraction than the required fuel—at least to the passengers! We all raced for the house phones to call our offices. But that chocolate cake beckoned; "Mom" knew how to bake, and no one appreciated it more than Walt Disney.

My second Gulfstream trip with Walt was made as an attempt to convince the Ford Motor Company to continue their successful New York World's Fair relationship with Disney by sponsoring an attraction the Imagineers had created for the new Tomorrowland at Disneyland that was slated to open in 1967. Walt pulled out all the stops. Not only did he have designers Claude Coats and Xavier "X." Atencio create a new show, he also had Dick and Bob Sherman, composers and lyricists for *Mary Poppins* and "it's a small world," write a special tune for Ford. I took the words and directed photographer Carl Frith in illustrating the song as if it were a TV commercial. It was called "Get the Feel of the Wheel of a Ford!"

> *Settle back—take command*
> *Hold tomorrow in your hand*
> *Get the feel of the wheel of a Ford!*
>
> *Feel the pride as you glide*
> *And you're envied and you're eyed*
> *Get the feel of the wheel of a Ford!*

Dream of a Dream Car
Just for you
Ford makes your Dream Car
Dreams come true

So to know how it feels
To have wings on your wheels
Get the feel of the wheel
Of a great automobile
Get the feel of the wheel of a Ford!

Claude, X., and I joined Walt in making the presentation to Henry Ford II. It was an all-out performance: we shipped the attraction model to Detroit and played the song we illustrated with lyrics sung by Dick Sherman. To showcase the song's versatility, we had three different versions—the "commercial" version, another where Dick imitated Maurice Chevalier, and another in country-and-western style. Then, of course, Walt talked about how successful Ford had been with the Magic Skyway show at the New York World's Fair: more than sixteen million people visited their pavilion over approximately two years, meaning about 33 percent of the fair's fifty-one million attendees rode in Ford convertibles through the Disney show.

When we were working on Ford's World's Fair pavilion, I once sat in while their advertising agency presented the first ad campaign for the storied Mustang, which made its debut at the fair in April of 1964. But I doubt whether Mr. Ford or his top executives had ever seen a more passionate or dynamic pitch for a corporate sponsorship—especially with one of the world's most famous entertainers taking an active part. Yet there was (to put it mildly) an almost ho-hum attitude from the head man of the Ford empire. He thanked Walt for coming to Detroit . . . and left almost immediately after the presentation. No discussion!

The Imagineering team was, of course, disappointed— but thankful that Walt had been with us to see how well we represented his team's efforts. But for Walt, it was almost a slap in the face. After all, he and his Imagineers had created a hit show for Ford at the world's biggest fair, and he had taken the time to fly across the country and join us for the presentation, showing his personal involvement and commitment.

Walt summed up his feelings when we were back aboard the Disney Gulfstream. "That," he informed us, "is the stupidest man I ever met." We rarely disagreed with the boss, and on this occasion, we were 100 percent in agreement.

By the way, we did not make the sale. Walt had even put up his personal $1 million fee, which Ford had paid for the use of the Walt Disney name at the World's Fair; it was to be forgiven and included as the down payment for Ford's participation in Disneyland. In contrast, General Electric did use that million-dollar name fee as part of their sponsorship of the Carousel of Progress, which moved from New York to open as part of the new Tomorrowland at Disneyland, where it played from 1967 to 1973. Then in 1975, the carousel moved again—this time to Tomorrowland at Walt Disney World's Magic Kingdom. The carousel is still revolving in Florida. In 2017, it celebrated its fiftieth anniversary, still going strong as the longest-running stage show in history!

There was one more trip in that Gulfstream One that remains vivid in my memory because of its importance to

The Walt Disney Company. At the request of editor Max Lark, I wrote about that trip in the Fall 2016 issue of Disney's *twenty-three Magazine*, celebrating the opening of Walt Disney World in 1971.

My story was called "Validating Walt Disney's Master Plan." Here is what I wrote:

> *Opening Day for me actually took place almost four years to the day before October 1, 1971.*
>
> *It was mid-October, 1967. The Disney Gulfstream One was very full leaving Burbank on a key research mission: Put the prime decision makers together and visit the Walt Disney World site, and significant resort hotels, and come home having settled important development issues.*
>
> *To this day I wonder how many top executives should ride together in one aircraft—and how lucky I was to accompany them. Chairman Roy O. Disney stayed in Burbank, but aboard the company's Gulfstream were Roy's two closest associates, Card Walker and Donn Tatum; the heads of Disneyland and the new Florida project, Admiral Joe Fowler and General Joe Potter; Imagineering's leader Richard Irvine and three of his top designers, John Hench, Marvin Davis, and Bill Martin; Disneyland Park Operations chief Dick Nunis; consultant architect Welton Becket, and three members of his staff, who would design the Contemporary and Polynesian Resorts; and me.**

---

* Note: All the Disney cast members have been honored as Disney Legends.

What did this trip have to do with the opening of Walt Disney World? Everything! Because after visiting hotels in Atlanta, Miami and Grand Bahama, we headed for Orlando—and controversy.

Only one hundred acres or so where the Magic Kingdom would be built had been cleared of trees and the dense foliage typical of central Florida wetlands. The key question: Was Walt Disney's hand drawn master plan really the "map" that should be followed in developing these 28,000 acres? What were the first hotel themes to be developed, and were they located in the key places? Without Walt's Epcot community, why not start development of this huge acreage—twice the size of Manhattan Island— closer to the main highway, Interstate 4, and reduce initial infrastructure costs?

The discussions, and arguments, were so intense that after two days, one major decision was made: We'd rent two helicopters—one to enable photographer Carl Frith to shoot film of the property, and a smaller craft to allow close up still photos. And to supervise the photographer, while everyone else returned to Southern California, someone would also be left "on site." Me.

During the three days that followed, the photographer and I crisscrossed the Walt Disney World property from north to south and east to west so many times we stopped counting the wild animals we could track from the air, and the beautiful Cypress trees we could count on the shoreline of Bay Lake and other natural bodies of water. More importantly, we "mapped" the property photographically from the air—creating visual research that became a key design tool for future development.

And most important in terms of design and development progress toward Opening Day, the pictures validated Walt Disney's hand drawn Master Plan, calling for prime resort and entertainment projects to begin in the north of the property, spreading south, east, and west as the campground, more resort hotels, additional park and vacation concepts, water parks, the sports complex, and shopping and dining areas grew to meet the incredible demand of visitors from the four corners of the world who visit Walt Disney World each year.

Nearly half a century later, the direction Walt Disney gave to Harrison "Buzz" Price to analyze and recommend the location for Walt's World still rings true: Stay away from the ocean and Miami—that's where everyone expects Disney to go. Put this "world" at the center of the state of Florida, where the highways cross and the tourists roam. And if you build it well, they will come.

That Gulfstream One went on to set a world record for that aircraft model, logging more than 8,800 flights, nearly twenty thousand flight hours, and approximately five million miles by the time it retired in 1992. For years it ferried Disney executives and other personnel back and forth between

Burbank and Orlando. Then it became a high-profile trans-porter for movie and TV stars featured in Disney and ABC-TV productions. And finally, it came to rest on the "back lot" of Disney's Hollywood Studios at Walt Disney World.

CHAPTER 2

TRICKS AND TREATS— TEN TALES OF TRAVEL

Travelling with Walt Disney was a treat and a thrill. But it was just the cherry on top of the whipped cream if you enjoy seeing the world—and getting to know airlines and airports around the world. In my travel time, it was a very different world—one in which the passenger was not overwhelmed by today's security concerns and airport pat-'em-ups (and downs).

So many experiences, so many adventures, so many stories to recall and tell. . . .

What follow are ten of my favorite travel-related adventures—from Los Angeles to Reykjavík, Iceland; from Orlando to Zermatt, Switzerland—as I travelled the world helping to make Disney dreams come true. I've started with an obvious title—so the numbering system may seem backward! But I couldn't resist starting with:

10. Air France Gets a 10

The Air France 747 began its acceleration down the runway. I had finished a week of reviews during the construction of what was then called Euro Disney, and is now Disneyland Paris. I was more than ready for a Johnnie Walker Black as soon as we were airborne.

Suddenly, as we seemed about to lift off, the aircraft slowed, finally coming to a full stop at the end of the runway. Something had signaled the pilot that there was a problem, and we were turning around. On a parallel runway, we returned to the terminal, where we would remain on board for more than an hour while the issue was resolved.

Bummer! Well, sometimes there are compensating circumstances . . . and this turned out to be one of those times.

When the passengers began to mix while we waited to fly, it turned out that just across the aisle from me was a striking blond woman I instantly recognized. I easily remembered the famous scene in the 1979 movie *10* featuring her jogging on the beach. Obviously, Bo Derek deserved every one of those numbers that added up to the quintessential sex symbol: she was indeed a "10." She had earned her reputation as a big-time movie star in that comedy, and luckily there was a Disney connection: *10* was directed by Blake Edwards, whose wife, Julie Andrews, had become an instant movie star in Walt Disney's *Mary Poppins.*

And it didn't take long for Bo and Marty to discover a common interest—Euro Disney. It turned out that Bo is a riding enthusiast—her autobiography is called *Riding Lessons: Everything That Matters in Life I Learned from Horses.* And the reason she was in France was to visit friends who were rehearsing the original Buffalo Bill's Wild West Show, a dinner show performed several times nightly in the Disney Village when Euro Disney opened.

So how many times does a flight delay rate a "10"? This one did! We had a long and lovely conversation about horses, Buffalo Bill, and the exciting park we were building that would later open on April 12, 1992, in Marne-la-Vallée, a French "new town" located thirty miles east of the center of Paris.

In writing this chapter, I knew it would be hard to top Bo Derek—after all, you don't easily top a "10." But there were many other highlight flights in my Disney career. So with Bo Derek a "10," here are nine more that rise to the top of my career travel memory bank.

9. Meeting General Omar Bradley

It was the first cross-country flight I ever made, predecessor of hundreds more during my years as an Imagineer—I estimate I have flown between Los Angeles and Orlando alone on Walt Disney World projects approximately 250 times!

John Hench was perhaps the greatest Disney designer—and in so many ways he was my number one mentor. This time we were on our way to New York. John was not just a Disney Legend—designer of Space Mountain and Spaceship Earth, Walt's selection to paint the first portrait of Mickey Mouse, and renowned for his knowledge of the use of color—he was also the bon vivant gentleman in our midst.

He became a close friend of Salvador Dalí while working with him on Dalí's original film, *Destino*, at Walt Disney's request. With his distinctive mustache, John was often mistaken for Walt—sometimes (to John's chagrin) while walking with Walt in Disneyland. Walt did not appreciate it.

Hench was easily the smartest person I knew. He seemed to be conversant on any topic. In my *Dream It! Do It!* book, I related how I once asked John's assistant, Sandy Huskins, to bring me all the books and magazines John took home one weekend. When they arrived on my desk Monday morning, I counted thirty-four books and magazines, ranging from *Scientific American* to *Women's Wear Daily* (John approved and often designed the costumes for Disneyland)!

John had another talent, which he used to his advantage on special occasions—such as to curry favor on cross-country flights: he read palms. He had mastered the technique because he truly believed in what those palm lines revealed to him.

I don't recall the kind of aircraft we flew on that New York trip, but I do remember the pretty flight attendant who was soon mesmerized by the tale of her future, as read and reported by Mr. John C. Hench. He had two simple requests as a quid pro quo: first an extra glass of Scotch for himself and his friend (me), and, second, could we both enjoy the small compartment between the galley and first-class seating—a kind of VIP hangout in those days?

And that's where we met the World War II hero and five-star general, Omar Bradley, and his wife, Kitty. What a thrill! I was in awe. And I was also thankful that John did not offer to read the palm of General Bradley's wife!

8. The Great Hat Pin Caper

One of the possessions John Hench was most proud of was a wonderful Alpine hat that he had worn to the 1960 Winter Olympics in Squaw Valley, California. John was a creative star at those winter games. Walt Disney, who was responsible for the pageantry and entertainment there, had called on his Disney team—designers at Imagineering, operators and the entertainment team from Disneyland—to work their magic.

John's assignment was to design the "snow statues" created to represent the major sports then in Olympic competition: skiing, hockey, figure skating, speed skating, etc. The international athletes loved them—and John. Soon his hat was covered with pins from many countries, all given to him by those grateful athletes. That hat became John's signature.

In the early days of Walt Disney World, the direct flight from Los Angeles to Orlando continued to Miami. One day in the late 1960s, when the Magic Kingdom was under construction, John left his hat in the overhead compartment when we debarked in Orlando. As you would suspect with all those Olympic pins in it, the hat became someone else's treasured souvenir—never to be returned to John.

I knew John was devastated by the loss. So I waited and waited—more than a year—to ask him whether he was going to start another "pin hat." "No," he told me, "it will never be the same for me."

Thus began my own venture into the world of pin collecting—and displaying those pins on my own hat. Every pin on my hat has a story to tell—there's a reason each one is there, when I have dozens and dozens more to choose from. So what follows is the story behind nine of my favorites from among the eighty that adorn my hat. Thanks again to John Hench for the inspiration!

Measuring Distance by "Sleeps"

Imagineering created a Circle-Vision 360° film called *Portraits of Canada / Images du Canada* for the Telecom Canada Pavilion at Expo '86 in Vancouver, Canada. It presented a look at the lives of eleven individual Canadians who were brought together for the expo's grand opening on May 2, 1986.

One Canadian featured was a member of one of the indigenous peoples of northern Canada, the Inuit. He was a musher by profession, leading dogsled teams, and he had lived his whole life in the Arctic. Until his trip to Vancouver, he had never been in an airplane, never been in a city, never stayed in a hotel. At the opening reception, he took one look at my hat and focused immediately on one thing he somehow knew: Donald Duck. His first questions (through an interpreter): What was Tokyo Disneyland? How many "sleeps" away was it? This was the way he measured distances—how far his dogsled could travel before he had to stop for the night and therefore sleep. With great pleasure, I gave him this pin—and replaced it on my next trip to Tokyo. So if you meet an Inuit dogsled musher wearing a Donald Duck pin from Tokyo Disneyland, you will have met one of the stars of *Images du Canada* from Vancouver's Expo '86.

ARC (Cuisine de Femmes)

During the building of Euro Disney (now Disneyland Paris) Leah and I had dinner one night somewhere in the countryside east of Paris. Our companions were Jim and Mimi Cora and Mickey and Marilyn Steinberg. Jim, the president of Disneyland International and the leading operations executive on the project, and Mickey, vice president of Imagineering, were heading our team's construction efforts in France. When the female chef came out of the kitchen and saw my hat full of pins, she immediately removed this pin from her chef's jacket and gave it to me. It reads: ARC—CUISINE DE FEMMES—the symbol of female chefs in France, who created their Association of Women Restaurateurs-Cooks when they were shut out of the male-dominated professional restaurant groups.

"Hands Across America"

Ken Kragen, a Hollywood entertainment manager and executive, organized the "We Are the World" gathering and song recording that brought together dozens of performers in 1985 to raise funds to fight starvation in Africa. Then, on May 25, 1986, he organized "Hands Across America," an event in which 6.5 million people linked hands for fifteen minutes in a chain "across America" to raise money to fight homelessness, hunger, and poverty. Leah and I joined friends to participate in Palm Springs, California.

Disney's Mickey and Goofy joined the hand-holding chain in Long Beach, California.

The Tournament of Roses Parade

One of my great treats was tied to Disneyland's fiftieth anniversary when I was asked to be a judge of the float awards for the 116th annual Tournament of Roses Parade in Pasadena, California. The date was January 2, 2005. (No parades are held on Sundays, which was when New Year's Day fell in 2005.) The theme was "Celebrate Family," and, in honor of Disneyland's fiftieth birthday that year, the grand marshal was Mickey Mouse himself. (Walt Disney had been the grand marshal of the parade on January 1, 1966.)

I was honored that the Rose Parade committee wanted a design representative from Disney to be one of the three judges of the national, international, and local floats participating in this annual extravaganza, broadcast live to twenty-eight countries around the world. We rated on a broad range of criteria related to flowers, design, and themes for the fifty floats in the parade—but not on the remarkable Disneyland entry, which promoted Disneyland's fiftieth birthday in a non-competing float representing "The Happiest Celebration on Earth."

We three judges were driven in a motor home to locations in and around Pasadena, where we viewed and judged the floats in various stages of preparation. What a treat to see the dedication of thousands of volunteers to create beauty and pleasure for the hundreds of thousands of viewers on the streets of Pasadena and millions of television viewers around the globe. As judges, we were on the move for three days, with a final look at the float lineup at 5:00 a.m. the morning of the parade. That was our last chance to see the beauty in the early light of day; fortunately, that last viewing did not change our award selections at all, but it did show us how intently the Tournament of Roses wanted to get it right before the kickoff for the parade.

And speaking of kickoffs, in one of the greatest Rose Bowl games of them all, the ninety-first annual gridiron battle was won by the University of Texas over the University of Michigan, 38–37, on a game-ending field goal.

Trust in Me

For me, as the creative leader of the Imagineers, this may be the most significant pin of the eighty or so on my hat. Here's how it was given to me: It was  another frozen day in Marne-la-Vallée, where Euro Disney was under construction. While my Imagineering partner, vice president Mickey Steinberg, led the building effort, I was on the site for a regularly scheduled review that had several objectives: first, to assure myself and Disney leaders in Burbank and nearby Glendale that the project was proceeding well; and second, to hopefully lift the spirits of the dedicated Imagineers working seven days a week in that cold, wet environment.

My chilly (read "frozen and wet") walk was almost over

when we approached John Olsen, a true hero of Disney park fieldwork around the world. (You can see John's skill on building facades, walls, and major features of the built environment in every Disney park. More than that, it was John, and a frequent partner, Skip Lange, who taught crews from Florida to Paris and Tokyo to China how to do it "the Disney way.")

"Marty," John said, "stop for a minute." We were not alone, meaning seven or eight people, all wearing hard hats and rain gear, came to a halt and paused in the rain. Pulling off his gloves, John reached into his pocket. "We want you to have this," John said as he handed me this pin, "because it's *you* we are always excited to see reviewing our work. The pin says it all. We would be pleased if you added it to your hat."

I'm very proud to wear TRUST ME on my hat, and now to share its meaning for the first time.

Epcot's Mission: SPACE

I've told the story in *Dream It! Do It!* about the birth of the Mission: SPACE project.

I had an open-door policy for my office. One afternoon, Imagineering designer extraordinaire Eddie Sotto stuck his head inside and said, "Marty, come out here in the hall for a minute."

Almost immediately, Eddie was lying on his back. "Imagine," he said as he held both arms upright, "that you are in a space capsule. I'm the pilot, and next to me is the rest of the crew—engineer, navigator, and commander. It's astronaut training and we're on a Mission to Mars."

That was it—an idea illustrated without an illustration! It was enough to start a conceptual process: we built a full-size Styrofoam model, showed it to Michael Eisner, worked together with an outside company to create a multiarmed centrifuge (centrifugal motion simulator), brought in astronauts to authenticate the experience, created an "Advanced Training Lab" as a postshow "game," convinced a sponsor to help fund the project, and opened the four-minute Mission attraction on August 15, 2003.

What I love about the pin is that the shuttle vehicle on it actually moves. Your mission has begun on Marty's hat!

The French Had a Word for It

Pin collectors love the opportunity to trade theirs for yours. It was prudent to carry extra Disney pins with me; they were always popular, especially when  someone in Europe or Asia could obtain a Disneyland or Walt Disney World pin without travelling to California or Florida.

This pin came my way on a flight from Tokyo to Los Angeles, after I had reviewed projects in development at Tokyo Disneyland. The French rowing team had competed in the XXIV Olympiad, the Olympic Summer Games in Seoul, South Korea, in September 1988. They were on their way home: Seoul to Tokyo to Los Angeles to Paris.

I love the pin, but unfortunately the French rowing team did not win a single race.

Bastille Day: 1789-1989

We had the good fortune to be in Paris on July 14, 1989, the two hun- dredth anniversary of Bastille Day. The Bastille, a medieval fortress and prison,  was the symbol of the tyrannical regime of King Louis XVI. The "mob" that stormed the Bastille on July 14, 1789, became the spark that ignited the revolution that overthrew the French monarchy, personified by King Louis and his wife, Queen Marie-Antoinette.

Bastille Day is celebrated in France like July 4— Independence Day—in America. There are fireworks and parades. We will never forget the one we saw on the street outside our hotel on July 14, 1989. Leah and I were staying in a small hotel on a side street adjacent to the Champs-Élysées, the historic avenue that's home to all major French celebra- tions, from military parades to the finish of the annual Tour de France bicycle race.

Suddenly, our room began to shake, rattle, and roll. To us Californians, it felt as though an earthquake had struck Paris. But when we looked out our window, we saw French military tanks rolling down our street on the way to the Champs- Élysées.

Here's what two innocent Americans imagined as they looked out on those tanks and French soldiers: the time Hitler's Nazi German army rumbled down those streets in June 1940 to occupy Paris until the City of Lights was liber- ated four years later in August 1944.

This pin reminds me of that experience, and what Bastille

Day means—not just to the French, but as a symbol of freedom for people everywhere.

Mickey's Peace Sign

If there were ever two symbols that belong together, I believe they are the sign for peace and the hand of Mickey Mouse. It might just be the happiest marriage on earth. I wear it with pride on my hat.

I only wish I could remember the reason it was created . . . but no one seems to recall why or when. So perhaps by including it in this brief review of the pins I wear on my hat, someone will help solve the mystery of its creation.

In the meantime, I am thrilled to wear a pin that characterizes Mickey's role in bringing love, happiness, and peace to families and audiences around the world. Mickey Mouse has played many roles in the ninety years since Walt created him in his first starring role, 1928's *Steamboat Willie*. "When people laugh at Mickey Mouse," Walt said, "it's because he's so *human*. To me, Mickey is a symbol of independence."

"I only hope," Walt reminded his staff, "that we never forget that it was all started by a mouse."

7. My Early Mardi Gras

I mentioned earlier how many times I made that Los Angeles to Orlando flight. It would have been one more, except . . .

The Epcot project, originally called EPCOT Center to

emphasize its central importance to the development of the Walt Disney World property, was nine years in the making before its opening October 1, 1982. We were all back and forth so many times during construction that I could almost do it with my eyes closed. Or so I thought . . . until one Sunday when, with seemingly tons of paperwork in hand, I boarded my morning flight to Orlando at LAX. Then I buried myself in those memos and reports—and we were in the air.

It wasn't long, however, before the voice of the captain filled the compartment. "We'll be landing in New Orleans at 4:35." New Orleans! I jumped out of my seat and all but knocked over the nearest flight attendant. New Orleans? "Yes, Mr. Sklar—where did you think we were going?"

Long story short: I was early by a few months for Mardi Gras. While I did enjoy those famous New Orleans beignets and complete more paperwork than I ever imagined, those four hours I spent in the New Orleans airport waiting for a flight to Orlando were some of the longest hours I ever spent. Especially when the story of Marty's inimitable focus made the rounds as "our leader's inimitable screwup"!

6. Flights of Fantasy: From the DC-3 to the Concorde

I'm quite sure we are a vanishing breed: those who have flown aboard *both* a DC-3 and the Concorde.

The Douglas Aircraft DC-3 was the airplane that made transcontinental and worldwide flights a reality. My sole experience aboard a DC-3 was a flight from Dearborn, Michigan, to Philadelphia while we were being "indoctrinated" by our Ford Motor Company associates as background for creating the Ford pavilion at the New York World's Fair. Although DC-3s could be configured for twenty-one to thirty-two passengers, there were only six or seven of us on the way to visit Philco, then a Ford subsidiary making, among other things, electronic systems for the space program.

Even though DC-3s had a maximum speed of only two hundred miles per hour, the trip was the most thrilling flight I was ever aboard. Those thunderheads we encountered were awesome to see—and awful to experience. Our craft was like a rubber ball being bounced up and down, up and down—for miles and miles—for what seemed like forever. Thank goodness we had not been fed before takeoff!

What a contrast to my two flights aboard the French Concorde! They were both associated with our Paris project. The first followed a helicopter tour of our site with Robert Fitzpatrick, President of Euro Disneyland, and a well-known writer assigned to do a magazine story on the Disney project: Carl Bernstein. Yes, that Carl Bernstein!

On this day, following our aerial tour of the Marne-la-Vallée project, the helicopter landed at Charles de Gaulle Airport, and we were taken as VIPs directly to the French Concorde. There were twenty Concordes, configured to carry 92 to 128 passengers, built in a joint venture between British Airways and Air France. In contrast to the two hundred miles per hour speed of a DC-3, the Concorde's maximum speed was twice the speed of sound, and when it broke the sound barrier, you felt it.

Here's the Disney connection: the first simultaneous landing of the British and French Concordes on side-by-side runways, at Orlando International Airport, occurred October 18, 1982, to celebrate the opening of the French and British pavilions at Epcot! The two aircraft touched down, less than two seconds apart, next to each other before thirty-five thousand spectators, myself included. Not bad for the end of a transatlantic flight at supersonic speeds!

The idea for this historic event, which was covered by media from around the world, came from Jack Lindquist. Jack and I were "partners" in so many Disney projects from the early days of Disneyland, when, Jack loved to say, "We were willing to try anything, because there were no precedents." Over time, his marketing acumen led to the great "gift giver" promotion for Disneyland's thirtieth anniversary, when every thirty thousandth guest entering the park won a General Motors car (attendance increased by three million that year); the "What are you doing next?" campaign that features Super Bowl MVPs announcing their immediate plans to visit a Disney park; and, as already noted, the Concorde caper.

Flying aboard the Concorde (the French insisted on the "e" at the end; the British despised it) was an amazing experience, despite the narrow seats and lack of food service—though who needed a meal when you were up and down in three hours?

But for me, as I think about those "bookends" between the DC-3 and the Concorde, I can only say "bon voyage"—and thanks for the memories.

5. The Matterhorn Is Real!

The *real* Matterhorn in the Swiss Alps blew me away. Here's how the road to Disney Dreams took me there:

The original sponsor of Epcot's The Land pavilion was Kraft. Not long after Epcot's opening, that company became Dart & Kraft . . . and finally the "participant" (Disney-speak for "sponsor") became Nestlé.

It wasn't long after that when Nestlé asked me, as the creative leader of Imagineering, to visit their R & D center in Vevey, Switzerland. Ultimately, I made four trips there, but it was the very first one that I will always remember.

My host, Nestlé R & D executive Helmut Traitler, asked me to arrive a day before we were to meet at the R & D Center so he and his charming wife could show me around a bit of their countryside. We started out early in the morning with Helmut driving, and soon we approached an open clearing in a beautiful Swiss meadow. There waiting for us was a *helicopter* . . . and in a moment we were airborne on a crystal-clear winter morning. Destination: Zermatt, the crown jewel of European ski resorts.

My hosts knew how to treat a guest for lunch on a Sunday afternoon: take him for a ride across Switzerland to the highest ski resort in the Alps!

That helicopter flight was indeed a once in a lifetime experience. There we were on a sun-drenched day gliding above glaciers and between twenty-nine snowcapped peaks, six of them over 13,100 feet high, topped by Mount Rosa at 15,203 feet. Nine of the ten highest mountains in Europe surround the valley where Zermatt village sits at 5,276 feet;

it's dominated visually, of course, by *the* Matterhorn—all 14,692 feet of it.

Naturally, I thought immediately of Disneyland, where the Matterhorn mountain towers 147 feet above Fantasyland, a one-tenth scale "snow"-capped version of its Swiss counterpart. The Disneyland Matterhorn was inspired by the Disney film *Third Man on the Mountain*. The film, starring Michael Rennie and James MacArthur, was released in theaters the same year the Matterhorn, with its thrilling bobsled runs, opened in Disneyland.

Recently I reread portions of Harrison "Buzz" Price's important book *Walt's Revolution! By the Numbers*, published by Ripley Entertainment in 2004. Buzz, who had done the site studies and recommendations for the locations of Disneyland and Walt Disney World, founded Economics Research Associates (ERA), and became chairman of the board of CalArts, wrote the following about the all-year project in California that Walt Disney proposed to create at Mineral King:

> *Walt's interest in winter resort development came out of family trips to ski areas in central California and the family trip to Zermatt in Switzerland, a place that strongly intrigued him. The things he liked about Zermatt were simple: a great mountain, no autos, entry by shuttle train, and dual season operation with a base development full of charm and activity in both summer and winter. The village at Zermatt reflected the qualities of a Disney style and ambience.*

Zermatt is a charming village without cars—there are no internal combustion engines; every vehicle is electric-powered. It's accessed only via train, cog railway, or helicopter. Climbing, hiking, and mountaineering, as well as skiing, are the most popular activities, but it's the charming village, with its chalets, winding alleys, and picturesque restaurants, that's a tourism "must." It was at one of those restaurants that my hosts had reserved our lunch—with, of course, a picture window view of the *real* Matterhorn.

That helicopter ride across the Alps into Zermatt was a true thrill. But the return flight, with the sun creating even more visual magic as it reflected off the Matterhorn and surrounding peaks, topped even the arrival. Wow!

Visiting Nestlé's R & D Center in Vevey was a fascinating experience, so much so that I returned with Imagineering colleagues on three other occasions. But none of these could ever surpass visit number one and those helicopter flights over the snowcapped Alps into and out of Zermatt. Thank you, Helmut!

4. "Rabbi Ragins Is on Vacation."

I've told this story before . . . but I still need to catch my breath after reliving that Matterhorn experience in Switzerland. And this next one is also one of my favorites.

We were on the Gulfstream One again, and for some reason we were unable to land at Grand Island, Nebraska, for refueling. So this time, we landed at the state capital, Lincoln.

I was very excited because my good friend from UCLA, Sandy Ragins, was leading his first congregation as the head rabbi. It didn't matter that it was a small congregation, primarily older, in a part of the country where it wasn't easy to find a good Jewish rye bread—it was Sandy's early step up the ladder of congregational leadership.

Sandy and I had been friends at UCLA. He was a frequent contributor to the pages of the *Daily Bruin* student newspaper as I progressed from sports to city editor and then editor in chief. Sandy's opinion pieces, what today would be called Op-Ed, were frequently about student, community, and national issues. It was a portrait of things to come when he returned to Los Angeles as the assistant rabbi to one of Southern California's best-known rabbinic leaders, Rabbi Leonard Beerman, at Leo Baeck Temple in West Los Angeles. Rabbi Ragins later became the chief rabbi of the Leo Baeck congregation, where he now enjoys rabbi emeritus status.

But this was 1964, and as soon as the Disney Gulfstream landed in Lincoln, I was off the plane and racing to the telephone to call my friend. I dialed his number, expecting to hear Sandy's voice when he answered my call. But the voice I heard was not Sandy's: it was the central telephone operator for AT&T in Nebraska's capital, and she was loud and clear in her message: "Rabbi Ragins," she intoned, "is on vacation."

I've often wondered what the message might have been if I had asked for the mayor of Lincoln, or perhaps the governor of Nebraska!

3. "Is *She* the Pilot?!"

The giant 1969 media event that for the first time detailed plans for Walt Disney World to a wildly eager press and television had ended. Following the media events, Leah joined me for a well-deserved vacation. It was Leah's first time ever in Florida, so we set out for a leisurely drive from Orlando, heading down the west coast and stopping overnight in Naples. The next day we drove across Alligator Alley in the Everglades to Fort Lauderdale, stopping overnight before going to the airport for our destination, Freeport and Lucaya on Grand Bahama Island.

I had visited Grand Bahama before, in 1967, on that first trip to Orlando I wrote about in that *twenty-three Magazine* article mentioned in Chapter 1. Disney had hired John Curry, whose family had run the visitor services at Yosemite National Park, including Camp Curry and the Ahwahnee Hotel, for many years. John had become the general manager of a Freeport hotel that had just opened, so our Disney delegation—which was inspecting vacation hotels in and around the Southeast United States—flew to Grand Bahama for an overnight stay.

It was an "interesting" experience. The hotel had just opened, and it lived up to the classic "whatever can go wrong, does go wrong" cliché. Two examples:

- When no one answered the telephone when we called from our rooms, John Hench and I checked out the main desk. Lo and behold, there was no one there—and the telephones were ringing off the hook, as they say. John and I stepped behind the desk and began to answer the calls: They were all from our colleagues requesting or complaining about something. Two of the Welton Becket architects accompanying us had been showering, with soap on their bodies, when the hot water stopped running. We suggested that they might remove the soap by taking a dip in the hotel's pool. Without another option, they took our advice and soon passed us on the way to their "rinse cycle."

- For another guest who approached the desk, we provided change so he could use the vending machine in the lobby. The change was easy to find—the cash drawer behind the desk was wide open!

It was an introduction for us to the laid-back attitude we found at the time in our introduction to the Bahamas—and, to a large extent, Florida, at least in my first visit there in 1967.

Now it was 1969, and what I remembered most about Grand Bahama was its natural beauty and the riot of colors in local housing we had observed. So I wanted Leah to enjoy what I had seen—resolving in my own mind that, two years later, the hotel would have addressed its training and operating issues.

But this is a chapter about travel, and that turned out to be the highlight of our trip *to* (not from) Grand Bahama. With my meager knowledge of airlines that flew to the Bahamas, I booked us on Florida Atlantic Airlines. We were departing from the Fort Lauderdale airport; when our flight was called, a woman in a tropical sport shirt took our tickets and those of the sixteen other passengers booked on our fight. That woman turned out to be a rather important person on our trip, and not just at the gate. She was also the pilot—highly unusual in 1969!

The short flight to Grand Bahama, little more than fifty miles off the Florida coast, was the true adventure of our vacation. The aircraft never soared high enough above the ocean that we lost count of the dolphins and flying fish we saw below us, as well as the people waving to us from small fishing boats plying those waters. We were thrilled that six of our fellow passengers were toting their scuba-diving gear. To us landlubbers, it seemed as though we could touch the top of the waves below, so we looked upon our fellow passengers, wet suits and all, as our safety net.

For the return flight, we discarded our Florida Atlantic tickets and flew the major airline that served the Grand Bahama–Fort Lauderdale route. From our seats high above the beautiful blue ocean, dolphins were mere specks far, far below.

Fast-forward: the chain of islands called the Bahamas includes about seven hundred separate islands and 2,400 cays, including one that has become the most popular stop for passengers aboard Disney Cruise Line adventures in the Caribbean: Castaway Cay!

2. The IBM Golden Circle Circuit

When Epcot became an instant hit at its opening on October 1, 1982, I began to receive invitations from corporations, associations, conventions, fan groups, etc. to come and talk about "How Disney Does It!" As a result of my leadership with John Hench in developing the concept and executing the new park's ideas, most of these invitations came to me.

I began by speaking in St. Paul, Minnesota, at the national convention of Science and Technology Centers; then, on the same trip, I was the keynote speaker at the Boston Art Directors' Club. But it was the next invitation that I really loved. It came from IBM.

In my *Dream It! Do It!* book, I related the story of how Jack Lindquist, then head of Disney parks marketing, and I had learned that IBM was turning us down in our proposal to sponsor Epcot's theme show, Spaceship Earth—and how AT&T vice president Ed Block had said yes to sponsorship in these colorful terms: "Tell IBM to go to hell!"

Many companies had reward programs for their top performers. In IBM's case, there were two such programs; I was fortunate enough to speak at both the Golden Circle and 100 Percent Club reward programs. The latter was aptly named: as a salesman you were "in" when you made 100 percent of your quota.

To become part of the Golden Circle, however, you needed to be in the top 1.5 percent of IBM salesmen around the world. Their Golden Circle reward: a trip to an exotic locale. Singapore, Monte Carlo, Hawaii, and Iceland were just a few I was aware of in the 1980s and 1990s.

In my experience, these were "no expense spared" rewards for the high achievers. Their sales forces enjoyed performances by stars like Diana Ross, Michael Douglas, and the Smothers Brothers, and talks by the likes of Pierre Salinger—White House press secretary under President John F. Kennedy—and author James Michener.

My first invitation was for a program at the famous Breakers hotel in Palm Beach, Florida, for the Golden Circle achievers from Europe. I was probably low person on the speaker roster, which featured Alexander Haig, secretary of state under President Ronald Reagan and White House chief of staff under Presidents Richard Nixon and Gerald Ford. The retired United States Army four-star general was obviously not used to interfacing with lowly civilians; he was aloof and mostly ignored his fellow speakers, me included. (Apparently, we forgot to salute when he entered the room.)

I don't recall much about the program I participated in on the Hawaiian island of Maui—except, of course, how beautiful it was in Kapalua and in the historic whaling village, Lahaina. Not so with my third and final Golden Circle adventure. Hawaii was warm and beautiful; but Iceland, my next IBM stop, was cold and awesomely exotic.

What a fabulous adventure! The speakers were invited to participate in the bus tours that the Golden Circle winners took. Leah accompanied me and we saw many of the natural features of the island: waterfalls, geysers, lava fields, glaciers, volcanoes.

Visually, it was an incredible treat . . . and when those tours whetted our appetite, we were fortunate to have a connection for further adventures. Leah's brother, Paul Gerber, had produced the wonderful film *Symbiosis*, which was a key feature of The Land pavilion during Epcot's first ten years. Paul had shot scenes for *Symbiosis*—a story of man's relationship with his environment around the world—in Iceland.

We hired part of Paul's Icelandic production team for a day, and in a four-wheel drive Jeep, we explored places even more remote than those the IBMers had visited. Most amazing were the rolling lava fields where our American astronauts had trained for landing on the moon; the area literally looked like the moonscape we have all seen in the video and photos transmitted from the moon by astronauts Neil Armstrong, Buzz Aldrin, and Michael Collins.

The nearby black sand beach was an amazing sight. But when I needed to change film rolls in my camera, my hands were so cold I could not pick up the roll I dropped—and lost forever. Oh, for that digital world to come!

One of the most interesting experiences was staying at

the Hotel Holt—not far from the Höfði House hotel where Ronald Reagan and Soviet president Mikhail Gorbachev had met in the Reykjavík summit in October 1986.

Part of the exotic nature of the Hotel Holt was the sulfuric smell of the water, the result of Iceland's geothermal energy, which took some getting used to. But what we could not get over was the amount of original art on display everywhere in the hotel—in every public space, including hallways, and in every guest room. It was a museum's worth of paintings and sculpture, some of it heroic in size, in bars and meeting rooms—all of it Icelandic subjects created by Icelandic artists. Finally I had to ask—and here's the explanation I was given: "Mr. Holt was the number one pig farmer in Iceland. He began collecting art created by Icelandic artists. When his collection grew too large for his farmhouse, he built Hotel Holt so he could display all of it."

Imagine—we were eating and sleeping in an art gallery/ museum! The only thing missing was a docent to lead us and tell stories about the museum-quality works of art! Together with the menu of mouthwatering fresh fish from the north Atlantic Ocean—salmon, Arctic char, and sea trout—that Hotel Holt environment remains in my memory as strong as the geysers and waterfalls of an incredible island.

Oh, and about the IBM Golden Circle: one of my fellow speakers was Monica Kristensen Solas, a Norwegian glaciologist and polar explorer. She had been the leader of an expedition to the South Pole tracing the route of her countryman Roald Amundsen, who in 1911 became the first person to reach the South Pole. Although Monica had been forced to turn back before reaching her goal, her experience left us with wonderful tales of adventure—somehow even more relevant when told in that Icelandic setting.

I loved it when AT&T's Ed Block agreed to sponsor Epcot's Spaceship Earth and suggested that we "tell IBM to go to hell." But by the time I came back from my third appearance at an IBM Golden Circle, I had another view and was more than happy to say, "Thanks, Big Blue!"

1. The Kodak Tragedy: Figment Yes, Digital No

All of us at Imagineering who worked with Eastman Kodak to create the original Journey Into Imagination pavilion in Epcot were thrilled to be part of the creation of one of the most enduring characters in Disney park history . . . and amazed to watch the demise of one of the world's great companies. The two experiences overlapped—just as we were creating Figment and his partner, Dreamfinder, Kodak received the patent for the very first "electronic still camera." As visitors learning about the world of Kodak for the Epcot pavilion, we were excited to learn about and meet the people who invented this amazing new technology.

The digital revolution in photography began in 1973 with a Kodak electrical engineer named Steven Sasson. By 1975, he had built the first digital camera (now on display in Washington, D.C., at the Smithsonian National Museum of American History). And by 1978 Kodak had the original patent for that all-electronic digital camera.

They were off and running with the future of digital

photography in their grasp. Except the Kodak marketers were petrified, fearing that digital photography would destroy their business model. Think of it: it was estimated at the time that with Kodak Instamatic cameras, Kodak film, Kodak processing and chemistry, and Kodak paper, Eastman Kodak at its zenith controlled 70 percent of the U.S. photo market.

Kodak's attachment to film, driven by this dominance of the market, blinded its management to the potential of digital imaging. They saw every digital camera sold—even as they profited, because they owned the patent—as a threat to film sales. All true . . . and the problem was, when their patent expired in 2007, they not only no longer received income from licensing their patented technology, but it came to a point where their film sales died. Digital had won—and Kodak was out.

In 2012, the great Eastman Kodak filed for bankruptcy. It was, in retrospect, one of the greatest tragedies in American business history.

Our purple dragon, however, lives on. He was invented in 1978, when the patent for Kodak's digital camera was granted. That decision by Kodak's management was a perfect and lasting one. Figment became the overarching symbol of the Kodak-sponsored Journey Into Imagination pavilion in Epcot, and the enduring sidekick of our creative team at Walt Disney Imagineering.

Kodak should have paid more attention to the words Richard Sherman and Robert Sherman wrote in our show's theme song:

> One Little Spark
> Of Inspiration

Is at the heart
Of all creation
Right at the start of everything that's new
One Little Spark
Lights up for you

That digital spark invented by Kodak indeed has lit up the world of photography. Unfortunately, it also put out the light of a business model of an American icon, more than a century after George Eastman founded the company in 1888.

CHAPTER 3

THE NEW YORK WORLD'S FAIR: FROM "MENOPAUSE MANOR" TO FLUSHING MEADOWS

In its promotional literature, the Dearborn Inn in Dearborn, Michigan, today describes itself as "reminiscent of Traditional American hospitality." This identification is enhanced by its seven self-described "colonial lodges and guest houses." For our Imagineering team, this is where the 1964–65 New York World's Fair began.

When we first visited the Dearborn Inn in 1961, my Imagineering associate John Hench gave it a nickname that seemed fitting at the time. He called it "Menopause Manor." It was not a compliment. Built in 1931 on the grounds of the Ford Motor Company, by 1961 the Dearborn Inn was experiencing a transformation in life, and it was not aging well. However, it was to be our "home away from home" for more than a few long weeks as our Ford mentors immersed us in a deep dive into their company—from its pioneering transportation history to its projected future role in space with subsidiaries Philco in Philadelphia, Western Development LAB in Palo Alto, and Ford Aeronutronic in Newport Beach.

I wrote extensively about developing the Ford pavilion for that world's fair in *Dream It! Do It!* For a much more detailed story, I refer you to that memoir. But I do have several stories I did not have space for previously that I want to share with you here.

Some background: when the dialogue between Disney and Ford began, the Imagineers proposed a show that would transport audiences to the Disney versions of the wonders of the American natural world—from the Everglades in the Deep South to the deserts of the American Southwest. The thing Ford loved was that—using the Disney-patented PeopleMover system that would become an attraction in the new Tomorrowland at Disneyland in 1967—we gave fair guests a seat in a Ford convertible to see the show. It was almost like a showroom on wheels. Visiting the scenic sites of America, though? It was just too close to "See the USA in your Chevrolet"—a slogan from perpetual rival General Motors. Even the dazzling illustrations by Herb Ryman that put you right into those exciting places would not save this one.

So from the beginning, the convertibles were in—but the show idea was out. What to do?

Not surprisingly, Walt turned to his favorite all-star artists, led by one of his famous "Nine Old Men" of animation: Marc Davis. Inspired by Marc's humorous sketches, the Imagineers "reinvented the wheel," beginning with the caveman who first determined that square was out and round was in when it came to designing wheels. Our story then simply followed where the caveman's invention led—as it freed him, his family, and civilizations that followed to move about, try new things, and expand our world until we reached for the stars.

And by the way, it was a great "rehearsal" for Marc Davis. His next assignment from Walt: the buccaneers of Pirates of the Caribbean!

While we learned all about the Ford Motor Company (everywhere we travelled, our efficient host John Sattler introduced us by telling his company associates that "Marty is taking copious notes"), we also had several side adventures of note. My personal favorite was a nightmare for John Hench—and only reinforced his conviction that our Dearborn Inn "home" was indeed "Menopause Manor."

Jack Sayers, Disneyland's vice president of corporate sponsorships, liked to stir the pot, so to speak. In other words, if there was a questionable choice to be made, Jack usually chose the option that got us in trouble.

We returned one night to Menopause Manor about 11:00 p.m. following a very wet dinner, and Jack headed straight to the bar—only to emerge a few minutes later to literally pull John Hench inside. There, occupying all the tables in the bar, were twenty-four women—members of the Trenton, Michigan, Pinochle Club on their monthly "night out." It had taken Jack only moments to convince those nice women that there was a true seer in the hotel who would "make their night" by reading their palms—all twenty-four of them!

And so it began for John. Not wishing to offend any of the women, he explored a palm from each one. It must have been a boring task for John—until number 22. That was when John suddenly sat up straight, looked directly at the lady, and said very quietly, "You're having trouble with your husband." And the startled woman immediately shot back, "How did you know?"

We never knew for sure, but we suspected that whoever held the winning pinochle hand, it was not that woman. The palm of *her* hand was occupied with other matters.

* * * * * * * * * *

I feel I must repeat one story from *Dream It! Do It!* here because it is so emblematic of what we experienced in travelling around the 1960s world of the Ford Motor Company. Here's what I wrote:

> *An interesting moment occurred when we visited Ford's "Advanced Styling" unit. When we found two designers working on reversible seat cushions, John asked them if either one had any inkling if the public was interested in this feature. "No," both designers responded. "Then why," John inquired, "are you doing it?" "Because we like it," they said. "Well," John pursued, "has anyone ever tried this before?" "Oh, yes," the designers answered. "It was on the last Packard ever built!"*

As I mentioned earlier in the "Travels with Walt" chapter, the Ford pavilion's Magic Skyway attracted sixteen million visitors, or 33 percent of the New York World's Fair's fifty-one million attendees for its two six-month seasons.

But for me, the greatest compliment was still to come . . . even though it took thirteen years after the fair's ending to receive it. The only pavilion in New York that outdrew Ford's at the fair was General Motors', which was bigger, and had even more ride capacity. GM was understandably very proud of it. But now it was 1978, and GM had just signed a contract to become the first major sponsor of an attraction in Epcot at Walt Disney World. And who do you think they wanted to create their pavilion's shows? The Imagineers, of course.

One thing I have learned over and over through the years: find the best talent you can afford and give them enough creative freedom to do their best thinking and design, and you have the best chance to "create magic." I don't know if "the proof is in the pudding." But it certainly is in the Disney parks!

* * * * * * * * * *

I'm quite sure that I spent more time working with General Electric as a participating sponsor in our Disney parks than with any other client.

It started at the New York World's Fair in 1964, moved on to Disneyland in 1967, crossed the country to Walt Disney World in 1975 (with the Carousel of Progress at the Magic Kingdom), expanded to Epcot's Horizons in 1983, and finally came to an end in 1993 at Epcot and 1995 at the Magic Kingdom. In the world of corporate relationships, thirty years is at least two lifetimes.

Of course, there are many reasons that a business/creative association lasts so long. GE saw that initial relationship with Walt Disney as a halo effect—a name and culture association worth far more than that $1 million fee they paid initially for the use of Walt's persona at the New York World's Fair.

Here's how it began: in 1960, GE and other manufacturers of heavy electrical equipment were indicted and convicted in court trials of price-fixing. The scandal rocked the industry and resulted in heavy fines. Two high-ranking GE executives were even sent to jail.

With the 1964–65 New York World's Fair sales effort underway, GE was easy prey for Robert Moses, the fair's president. In GE's case, they had a reputation to rebuild; we were told that in a 1959 survey, 80 percent of the public in the New York area responded that they did not trust GE.

Participation in the New York World's Fair was a given for a major corporation of GE's status. But what could they do to repair their image?

That's when GE turned to that friend of the family who came into your home on Friday (and later Sunday) nights on ABC with one of television's most popular shows, *Walt Disney Presents*. Could "Uncle Walt" wave his magic wand over GE and repair that price-fixing reputation the company still couldn't shake?

Fast-forward once more to 1965, following the two years of the New York World's Fair. Progressland, the General Electric pavilion with its not-so-subtle name relationship to Disneyland, was a huge success. Its Disney shows, anchored by the Carousel of Progress, had also attracted nearly sixteen million visitors, over 33 percent of the fair's fifty-one million attendees, which was almost exactly the same numbers enjoyed by the Ford pavilion.

Walt loved that Carousel of Progress show, with its visits to four average homes to see family life in the pre-electric 1890s era, the 1920s, the 1940s, and "today" (filled with GE products of every period, of course). And the public loved Father (our narrator), Cousin Orville in his bathtub, the family dogs . . . and, once more, GE. As the fair came to an end,

GE repeated that same survey in the New York area, and this time, 80 percent of those questioned *approved* of GE! The number one reason for that dramatic turnaround? GE believed it was their association with one person. His name, of course, was Walt Disney.

As you can imagine, GE was anxious to continue that association with Walt and the Imagineers. Disneyland's new Tomorrowland was the first stop, in 1967. Unfortunately, Walt was gone at the end of 1966. But the bond had become so strong that the relationship lasted almost three more decades.

One result was that some of my personal favorite corporate associations were executives at GE. We always enjoyed dealing with Dave Burke, manager of corporate communications; Jim Rebeta, his financial partner; and Ned Landon, a wonderful journalist-scientist representing the GE scientific team in Schenectady, New York.

Burke was especially interesting to us, and to Walt, because he had been a key GE corporate liaison to the *General Electric Theater* television show. During his eight years as host of the show during the 1950s and early 1960s, Ronald Reagan had become a spokesman for GE; and as he made speeches to GE's workers, he was transforming from a "B" Hollywood actor into a political advocate for conservative causes. Although the relationship ended in 1962, many credit Reagan's political success to the base he was able to build with GE.

I was fortunate to develop good friends at many companies we worked with. Long after our formal relationships had ended, even though Disney no longer had an official connection to their companies, I continued to keep my corporate friends informed about what The Walt Disney Company was doing—especially in the Parks and Resorts business. Fortunately, I was often rewarded with their appreciation and thanks.

I especially treasured one of those rewards, a letter in 2003 from Dave Burke—almost ten years after our contract with GE expired.

October 11, 2003

Dear Marty,

This is an inexcusably long-postponed letter of appreciation for your many mailings on Disney news. After your most recent plug for the Carousel of Progress (Uncle Orville and the heat), I knew the time had come.

I follow the Disney doings in the New York Times— e.g. John Hench at age 95 resourcing their Disney-Dalí story, and the occasional obit about people like Marc Davis, as well as the usual business news about the company as it happens. But your mailings give me the "insider" look that I welcome because of my continuing interest in Walt's company and what's doing with you.

After 40 years at GE and association with creative leaders in many media, you, Marty, are among my top ten. Probably because I always felt comfortable working with you, more than with others. The very fact that you have kept in touch after decades since our last professional association, makes you unique. And speaking of uniqueness, I reckon that you—and only you—are the sole surviving associate of Walt still working at Disney.

So, Marty, what more can I say other than to thank

you most sincerely. As Walt would have it, you're my "wienie"—that one element that makes a production come to life. And speaking of Walt, I will never forget the incident when the first GE facility was under construction at Disneyland and Jim Rebeta and I were being shown around. As we were leaving, Joe Fowler took me aside and asked me, "Dave, do you think that as Walt looks down on us he approves of what we are doing?" I told him "yes indeed he does." So now I tell you, Marty, (without your asking) if Walt were to look down and ask me (which he wouldn't) if I approved of what Marty Sklar has done for Disney, my answer would be (to put it crudely): "You bet your ass I do!"

Sincerely,

Dave

Since we're talking about GE, there was much more to come in our relationship after the New York World's Fair.

As wonderful as our association was with Dave Burke, we knew our working relationship with GE had changed the day we met the company's new chairman-to-be, who would be the decision maker on their Epcot pavilion.

We had arranged to make our "final" concept presentation to Chairman Reginald Jones, who was retiring in 1981 after nine years as CEO. When the GE executives arrived, however, Jones was not alone. He was accompanied by GE's three vice-chairmen—the final candidates competing in a contest for Jones's job, with the selection soon to be made by the GE board of directors.

One of the three princes-in-waiting was extremely critical

of our proposal. When Chairman Jones made it clear that the new chairman would have final say on the pavilion plans, we held our breath until the GE board made its choice. Of course, the vice-chairman who did *not* like our concept was chosen. Jack Welch was to become a new kind of GE headman—and we became an early "victim" of his remaking of General Electric.

Although he did not invent it, "Six Sigma" became Chairman Welch's signature program in redefining GE. Company literature describes it as "a highly disciplined process that helps focus on developing and delivering near perfect products and services."

Unfortunately for us, in Jack Welch's mind, our concept was not "near perfect." In fact, it was 100 percent back to the drawing board—to the point that we could no longer make the October 1982 opening date for EPCOT Center. GE's new pavilion eventually opened a full year later.

The good news is that we now had the time—and the demand from the new chairman—to create something brand-new for Epcot. It was called Horizons.

Good stories, we are told, have a beginning, middle, and end. In Epcot's pavilions, we usually strived for that format: preshow, main show, postshow (especially with our major sponsors). But right from the beginning when he rejected our original concept, Jack Welch was a contrarian. He wanted one experience: get on board, enjoy the ride-show, thanks for coming, bye-bye.

In a General Electric promotional booklet, a story entitled "Disney's House of Magic" described the Horizons project this way:

The ride would include a whimsical look at past visions of the future; motion pictures of present day science and technology presented in Omnisphere, the world's largest motion picture system; and sets depicting Audio-Animatronics figures in different habitats of the future.

In the same story, I was quoted as follows:

Horizons is the type of pavilion that I think Walt had in mind when he visualized Epcot. It's a synthesis of all the other pavilions in that it encompasses energy, transportation, communications, and so on. And it incorporates a lot of "firsts" for us as a company. How do you start out interpreting a corporate culture? Our job was to create a pavilion specifically for GE, whose theme is "the achievable future." How do you bring that vision together?

Here's how: Horizons told its entire story in one ride-through, focusing on the theme of choice in *your* future; you could even choose the ending for the ride itself in onboard sound. As Imagineering's key show designer George McGinnis put it: "Both Disney and GE were anxious to show that desert, seas, and space could be interesting and practical places to live and work. . . . We're convinced that even though environments will change, people won't. . . . We believe one of the main differences high technology will make is that it will give us more choices."

That was certainly a theme of Walt's, and an objective for Epcot—in many ways, our version of a world's fair. As a GE executive expressed it, Horizons was "a vision of the future firmly rooted in what we know can someday be done. . . . Disney calls it 'Imagineering—If we can dream it, we can do it.' At GE, it harkens back to Thomas Edison's philosophy that it takes a little inspiration, and a lot of perspiration."

Jack Welch made sure that Horizons met his objectives by appointing Len Vickers, GE's vice president of corporate marketing, as our show liaison. Imagineers had to overlook Welch's description of his key aide: "Len is like an unmade bed." But he became one of our team, pushing us to achieve his company's (and the boss's!) directive: "The message implicit in Horizons," Vickers said, "is [this]: with the science and technologies already at hand, today's dreams *can* become tomorrow's reality. Any society that doesn't try to stretch its horizons is destined to see themselves shrink."

It's a pretty nice way to summarize that step from Disneyland to the New York World's Fair . . . and that leap from the Magic Kingdom to Epcot at Walt Disney World!

* * * * * * * * * *

Postscript

Unfortunately, the Horizons pavilion lasted only six years after GE's sponsorship ended in 1993. Today I believe it's the single most "missed" attraction in the listing of Epcot pavilion shows that are no longer running. As one inspired fan expressed it, "Horizons for me was *the* park attraction that triggered an understanding that entertainment can be art."

For me, the greatest loss of the Horizons pavilion was

the disappearance of Robert McCall's mural, *The Prologue and the Promise*. Without a postshow to *encumber* us (thank you, Jack Welch!) we needed some kind of "kiss good-bye" for our guests. We hired Bob McCall, who was known far and wide as the artist who epitomized the Space Age with his *Space Mural—A Cosmic View* at the National Air and Space Museum on the National Mall in Washington, D.C. He also created conceptual paintings for *2001: A Space Odyssey* and joined author Isaac Asimov to produce a book about space.

McCall and his wife, Louise, spent six months painting the nineteen-by-sixty-foot *The Prologue and the Promise* mural. Bob said it represented "the flow of civilized man from the past into the present and towards the future."

When GE's sponsorship terminated, we made plans to remove this incredible work of art. It had been a labor of love for Bob McCall—he even painted his family and family dog in the mural. So we arranged to carefully and safely remove the art, which had been painted on canvas at Imagineering in California and then rolled up and shipped to Florida for installation in 1983. Now it was time to make the return journey in the same manner.

Except—it never arrived. You would be amazed at how many times, and in how many ways, I personally requested a search and rescue operation. Imagine our embarrassment: a multimillion-dollar mural simply disappears?! And when Bob McCall called to inquire about what we planned to do with his work of art—a masterpiece that, between design and execution, had occupied ten months of his life—guess who had to explain to the artist that his mural had gone missing and might never be found? Me, of course.

Did you ever have to explain to your parents that you had lost your lunch money? Try finding a way to tell the person who had spent almost a full year of his life "creating magic" that the spell was over—the slipper no longer fits, because it can't be found. And to this day, it is still missing.

As one guest wrote on viewing *The Prologue and the Promise* at the exit to Horizons, "This work of art connects so beautifully to the original Epcot promise. . . . I just wanted to cry."

Me too.

CHAPTER 4

"I MAY NEVER BE FOUND ALIVE!"

Those 250 trips I estimate I've made between Los Angeles and Orlando are full of so many stories that it's hard to know where to begin. So I'll start by passing the baton to Jack Lindquist.

This chapter heading is the way Jack often retold the story of his first experience on the property Disney had acquired for what became Walt Disney World. It was early 1968, and Jack was getting his feet wet—quite literally—on the twenty-eight-thousand-acre property, sixteen miles outside Orlando.

I had instructed Jack on how to find us on the construction site:

1. Make sure you have a four-wheel drive vehicle. You don't want to get stuck in the mud if it rains.
2. Get a key to the gate located off I-4, on Florida Highway 192.

3. After you open and then "re-close" and lock the gate, drive north for about five miles.
4. Watch out for wild animals—the gators, snakes, and four-footed creatures still own this playground!
5. When you come to the area where land is being cleared for the Magic Kingdom, you are "home." Find us!

That's exactly what Jack Lindquist had been worried about—finding us. Or even more daunting, being found at all if he got lost. Because between that gate on Highway 192 and the beginnings of the Magic Kingdom five miles away, there was *nothing*! Well, nothing but wetlands, scrub oak, grassy fields, cypress head, and those creatures just noted of the land and water—depending on how far off the beaten path you strayed. Which was also what Jack worried about; if he missed the vehicle tracks in the pathway leading to our location, would he ever see his family again—let alone us?

I often think of "Jack's peril" when I visit Walt Disney World today and see there are thirty-five thousand hotel, campground, and vacation club places to stay . . . along with four Disney fun parks, two water parks, and three eighteen-hole golf courses . . . plus the ESPN sports complex, Disney Springs, and more places to eat than I can imagine. There's also a virtual city of backstage services to support the more than three hundred thousand visitors and Disney cast members who populate "The Vacation Kingdom of the World" on a typical peak day.

As the vice president of Disney Parks and Resorts marketing before he closed his career as president of Disneyland in 1995, that same Jack Lindquist had led the advertising and publicity efforts that brought *billions* of guests to Walt

Disney World. Jack had spent so many years counting the number of guests who passed through the Disney turnstiles that the idea of being alone in a Disney world must have frightened him more than any native animal you could name.

* * * * * * * * * *

Every one of us involved in the creation, building, and growth of Walt Disney World over its nearly fifty years has his or her own stories to tell. Here are a few more of my favorites:

In 1964, several Disneyland cast members were sent to Central Florida incognito for one purpose: validate the traffic information we were given by state and local sources. This, of course, was a key to our planning efforts—and even more, to assuring the Disney board of directors about the potential audience for such an endeavor. Some of the data our advance team returned with was not reassuring. One morning they counted *four cars* passing the intersection of Florida Highway 192 and the major interstate, I-4, between 10:00 and 11:00 a.m. Today that is the major entry to the Walt Disney World property; on a typical day, several thousand vehicles pass that intersection.

My second trip to Central Florida brought with it two revelations and lessons I never forgot. My travelling companions (Disney creative artist and animator T. Hee and Pete Clark, the Disney parks supersalesman in sponsor relations) and I arrived in Florida on a spring day in 1968. We had read and believed the tourist brochures about "sundrenched Florida," and were dressed appropriately—or so we thought. But the day we arrived, we learned that *Central* Florida could be *cold*—in fact, on our first day, it was thirty-two degrees, otherwise known as "freezing." We were.

We had set up a date to meet and convince the Florida Citrus Commission, located in Lakeland, to sponsor the Enchanted Tiki Room and a food facility in what would be Adventureland in the Magic Kingdom. Not being familiar with Florida, we arrived a day early and the next morning inquired about the attractions in that part of the state. The three greatest, we were told, were Cypress Gardens, made famous by its water ski shows and Esther Williams's film and TV specials of the 1950s and 1960s; the Singing Tower at the Bok Tower Gardens, a 205-foot-tall art deco tower that's home to a sixty-bell carillon that "sings" out over gardens designed by Frederick Law Olmstead, who also designed New York's Central Park and San Francisco's Golden Gate Park and is considered "the father of American landscape architecture"; and finally something called The Great Masterpiece. Knowing nothing about this attraction except that it and the Bok Tower were closest to Lakeland near Lake Wales, Florida—about thirty miles from the Walt Disney World site—we headed for Lake Wales.

I still shudder when I recall those short-sleeve shirts and light jackets we Californians were wearing on that thirty-two-degree day, but we were determined to see this special experience. Once we arrived at that last site, a woman in a warm winter coat sold us tickets and directed us to cross a grassy expanse (wet, of course) and have a seat on one of the two benches in front of a wall, about the size of a medium-scale movie theater screen, hidden behind a curtain. The show, she said, would begin promptly at 11:00 a.m. There was no literature, no explanation of what was to come.

At 10:58, that same woman, now smoking a cigarette, walked slowly across that grassy expanse, threw her cigarette to the ground (and stepped on it), approached the wall, checked her watch, and, at precisely 11:00 a.m., pressed a hidden switch. Thus began "The Great Masterpiece."

First, a voice dramatically began to tell us what a grand achievement "The Great Masterpiece" was—how many had worked to create it, how it was built with three hundred thousand pieces of glass mosaic tiles. . . . Then, as our curiosity and wonder peaked, the voice explained that it was based on the artistry of the great Leonardo da Vinci. "Now," the voice implored, "please join me in appreciation of this amazing experience."

This was the signal for the curtain covering "The Great Masterpiece" to open, slowly, with a full chorus of creaks as it revealed the whole mosaic, left to right. There in all its Lake Wales glory were those three hundred thousand pieces of mosaic, depicting Leonardo's *The Last Supper*.

I believe the entire experience lasted around five minutes. Then our charming hostess returned and pressed that switch again, this time closing the curtain; cue more creaks.

Since we were alone—the only three people in the audience—she thanked us for coming and invited us to shop for souvenirs in the merchandise store. It was the only way out.

We had just experienced what reportedly was one of "the three great attractions" in Central Florida in the late 1960s. T. Hee, Pete, and I came away believing that, somehow, Walt had found a location where his new Magic Kingdom would compete successfully with the local attractions.

That trip to Lakeland had a lasting impact that none of us could anticipate: the creation of Orange Bird.

Pete Clark was successful in signing a contract with the Florida Citrus Commission; they became the sponsor of the original Enchanted Tiki Room show and the Magic Kingdom's Sunshine Tree Terrace in Adventureland. One condition of making the deal: Disney agreed to create a new character as host of the attractions and "spokesbird" for Florida citrus.

My good friend and longtime collaborator, Disney Legend Robert "Bobby" Moore, the clever art director for the Walt Disney Studios' Publicity Department until his retirement in 1983, was up to the task. I had worked often with Bobby from the 1950s through the 1970s. We created everything from Disney annual reports to Walt Disney World promotional material and the Disney presentation for Mineral King.

Bobby had a pixie sense of humor. His Orange Bird was a lovable character, friendly and full of fun. It immediately took on a life of its own, first as the host of Sunshine Tree Terrace, and then as a walk-around character in the park, before finally becoming a star of books, records, and Florida citrus advertising—originally accompanied by singer Anita Bryant.

After the Citrus Commission sponsorship ended in 1987, the Orange Bird went into retirement, only to make a comeback at Tokyo Disneyland and, more recently, at Walt Disney World, especially as the star of vintage character merchandise. I began to receive requests—maybe a dozen—from "kids"; well, at least I *thought* they were from kids. They requested that I do a sketch of the Orange Bird for them. I had always refused to do sketches. But the Orange Bird is easy to draw—he's one big circle with oval eyes. So I sent back a Marty sketch to half a dozen or so "kids," until one day a friend called to say he had seen a drawing of the Orange Bird "by Marty Sklar" on eBay! Of course, I stopped doing drawings immediately. After all, the seller only wanted $150 for it!

One more note about my friend Bobby Moore: in September 1968, the United States Postal Service issued the Walt Disney commemorative stamp in Marceline, Missouri, where Walt spent a formative part of his boyhood. The stamp, featuring an image of Walt surrounded by celebrating children from countries around the world, was designed by Robert Moore, with finished art by another Walt Disney Studio staff member, Paul Wenzel. When issued, it was a full value postage stamp that cost six cents.

* * * * * * * * * *

If the actual Johnny's Corner had not existed, someone would have needed to invent it, or Walt Disney World might not have been built!

In an October 1965 press conference, Walt and Roy O. Disney joined Florida governor Haydon Burns to reveal that Disney was the purchaser of all that Central Florida land. According to the author of the Disney history blog *Passport to Dreams Old & New*, the announcement "set off a land speculation in Orlando frankly only comparable to a gold rush."

At the corner of Florida Highway 535 and Vineland Road, Johnny's Corner became a local institution because, *Passport* continues, "it was the nearest place to cash a paycheck and buy a beer." And in 1970, the *Palm Beach Daily News* reported:

At Johnny's Corner a man can get pig knuckles with his beer, a fan belt for his car, a can of snuff, a pair of used socks, a Barlow knife, or a Hong Kong suit "made to measure" for $49. He can cuss loud, peel eggs, play pin ball, argue about the union, eat sardines out of the can and hand wrestle by the gas pumps.

If the late Walt Disney didn't stop by Johnny's Corner when he was staking out land for his vacation resort, he should have. You get the feeling that the old master of folk lore would have liked this dirty old country store.

I remind readers about it now because in that ninety-degree summer heat, we probably could not have built the original Walt Disney World project without a Johnny's Corner. As the *Palm Beach Daily News* reported, "The customers at Johnny's Corner are brawny men with Mickey Mouse decals on their hard hats. They are the working men who are not allowed in the executive cafeteria on the Disney site about a 'country mile' away."

"If we tried to fix this place up they'd quit coming," the newspaper quoted Bill Waring, a co-owner. "These construction workers come in here dirty and they want the place dirty."

As you might expect, Johnny's Corner, an institution on Vineland Road for over four decades, eventually disappeared, replaced by a "modern service station." But before that, "there was even," *Passport* reveals, "a murder onsite in August 1981 during the construction of EPCOT Center." The *Gainesville Sun* write-up of the incident "painted an ugly picture of construction workers with nowhere to go but argue behind an old country store."

* * * * * * * * * *

So many important events surrounded the building, opening, and ongoing activities of the Contemporary Resort that I'll try to cover some of my most compelling memories.

Walt's Epcot philosophy really manifested itself in the construction of the Contemporary. In the original "Epcot Film" from 1966, Walt made several key points in reaching out to American industry to participate: that Epcot would be "a showcase to the world for the ingenuity and imagination of American free enterprise" and that "no one company can do this alone." One company that responded was U.S. Steel. They agreed to partner with Disney on the building of two hotels, the Polynesian Village and the Contemporary. The key to U.S. Steel's connection to the Epcot philosophy: all the rooms would be built at an off-site facility by a new method called "modular construction." As much of each room interior as possible—electrical, mechanical, plumbing, air-conditioning systems, and even mirrors and sliding doors—was installed three miles away. Then the units (weighing nine tons each) were transported to the A-frame Tower and lakeside buildings and "slid into place like drawers in a chest of drawers." The fourteen-story Tower building's outer walls contain 383 of the hotel's 655 rooms.

But the partnership between Disney and U.S. Steel would not endure. Before the end of 1971—three months after Walt Disney World opened—Disney bought out the U.S. Steel interest in the two modular hotels. The off-site facility (which was actually located on Walt Disney World property) was closed forever. The business of modular construction U.S. Steel had hoped to demonstrate with the Contemporary Resort was no longer viable on that scale.

The original press release from U.S. Steel, issued on December 8, 1970, referenced "the A-framed Tempo Bay Hotel."

Let me explain. John Hench and I were concerned that "Contemporary" was really not a name—it was a working title. So we created an elaborate and—in our view—beautiful graphics package for the name we liked: "Tempo Bay Resort."

Roy O. Disney listened to our passionate pitch and reasoning very patiently. When our presentation was finished, he thanked us, but dismissed our idea with one sentence: "What's wrong with Contemporary?" Careful how you label your "works in progress." They have a way of following you home.

The joke that was almost not funny went like this: "Without the Monorail, it would look like a place the Goodyear Blimp comes to mate." Yet, midway through the design, the two Welton Becket architects responsible for the project asked for a meeting with John Hench. Subject: removal of the Monorail from the project. After stating their reasons, Hench—in disbelief—asked the architects to sign a statement registering their "threat" to resign from the project. End of meeting. No signature. Monorail in. The Goodyear Blimp found another place to mate.

* * * * * * * * * *

The closest hotel/motel to the Walt Disney World site through much of our early construction was called the Gold Key. We knew we were not in Hollywood anymore when we overheard our housekeeper telling her friend that she was taking care of "the moving stars." We kept moving.

* * * * * * * * * *

Training cast members assigned to work in a hotel the size and scale of the Contemporary Resort was a massive undertaking. An important consideration was dealing with "real people." That's why, two weeks before opening day, many of us staying in other hotels were asked to move into the lakeside wings of the Contemporary.

The location was great—we were on-site, wherever we were working. But we quickly discovered why there was so much near and actual panic about whether the Contemporary Resort would be ready for its national television debut with the rest of Walt Disney World on October 29, 1971.

Today, with Central Florida one of the primary destination resorts in the world—thanks to Disney and Universal, its chief competitor in the themed entertainment business—it's hard to imagine that there was a lack of skilled workers in the late 1960s and early 1970s in the region. Finishing any project on time, let alone finishing it as designed, was more than a challenge—it was "hold your breath time" every day and in every way. And the very worst construction project on the entire Walt Disney World site was the Contemporary Resort.

In many ways, my Disney colleagues were the fortunate ones—all we had to worry about were things like this: Would our room keys work? Would there be lights at night? Would there be water in our bathrooms? Would there be *hot* water for our showers? (The pools were not finished, so in contrast to our hotel experience on Grand Bahama, we could not wash off the soap outdoors.)

The crew that somehow brought the Contemporary to a semblance of completion for opening day and the national TV show a month later was known as "Nunis's Raiders," in honor of the organization brought together by Dick Nunis, vice president of operations, to plaster, paint, and landscape a finished look almost overnight. There was still much to do, but when Bob Hope stepped off the Monorail to "one-line" the dedication, the guests were largely unaware of the issues.

And Hope won the day with lines about "sharing his bathtub with Donald Duck" and a remark that "Ponce de León couldn't find the Fountain of Youth, so Walt Disney created it." And in a serious vein, "Walt's dream is just beginning. I think you might want to tell your grandchildren you were there when it happened."

It was Mary Blair's mural that saved the day, every day, for all of us. I profess that I'm in love with Mary Blair's art. I keep a copy of the 1951 Little Golden Book she illustrated, *I Can Fly*, on my desk to remind me how beautiful and inspirational a story can be told simply in words (by author Ruth Krauss) and illustrations (by Mary Blair).

Mary Blair's ninety-foot-tall mural in the Contemporary Resort—eighteen thousand individual hand-painted ceramic tiles, fire-glazed, each one-foot square covering the fourteen-story elevator complex—remains today a triumph of style and beauty. Mary's playful imagination as a story-teller, and her amazing use of color, brought the mural to life as the centerpiece of the hotel. In fact, her theme and design of dramatic shapes, stylized birds, animals, flowers, and Southwest Native American children gave my team the inspiration for all the original resort nomenclature: Grand

Canyon Concourse, El Pueblo Room, Outer Rim (a bar), Grand Canyon Terrace, and Terrace Café, and several other places within the structure and surrounding grounds.

Small wonder that Dick Irvine, as the design chief of Imagineering, asked Mary Blair to conceive this mural. Walt had asked her to create the design of scenes and animated children around the globe for "it's a small world," and then the two fifteen-by-fifty-four-foot tile murals flanking the corridor at the entrance to Disneyland's new Tomorrowland. And who can forget Blair's styling in so many of the Disney animated films of the 1940s and 1950s such as *The Three Caballeros*, *Song of the South*, *Cinderella*, *Alice in Wonderland*, *Peter Pan*, and *Make Mine Music*?

"A bird can fly. So can I." Pardon me while I open that Little Golden Book once more and marvel at Mary Blair's little golden girl swinging high, toward the sky . . . reminding us that "I can play. I'm anything that's anything. That's MY way."

* * * * * * * * *

The location of the Contemporary Resort was carefully chosen by the Imagineers with the knowledge that the Tower structure would be seen from inside the Magic Kingdom park. Just as parts of the Polynesian Village can be seen from Adventureland's Swiss Family Treehouse, the Contemporary serves as a background for Tomorrowland. In fact, one of the most iconic visuals at Walt Disney World is a photo juxtaposing Space Mountain inside the Magic Kingdom and the Contemporary Tower building outside.

* * * * * * * * *

Still one more crisis occurred at the Contemporary Resort during the opening weeks. Bob Lane, Goodyear's vice president of public relations and corporate advertising, had signed the contract to sponsor the Grand Prix Raceway in the Magic Kingdom. Arriving late one night at the Contemporary, he was afraid he might not find a restaurant still open at the hotel, so he had picked up a chicken dinner off-site, and left it in his car while he unpacked his luggage and prepared to settle in for the evening.

Remembering his chicken dinner, he called for his car at the valet park . . . only to discover that his dinner was no more. The valet parkers were hungry, too!

* * * * * * * * * *

Among the many momentous occasions that have occurred at the Contemporary Resort since its opening, this is one for the history books: on November 17, 1973—during the height of his (and the nation's) Watergate crisis—President Richard Nixon spoke at the Contemporary Resort to four hundred managing editors of the Associated Press news service. "People have to know," he said in his speech, "whether or not their president is a crook. Well, I am not a crook!"

On August 8, 1974, the thirty-seventh president of the United States of America resigned. A scandal at another hotel, the Watergate in Washington, D.C., had taken its toll on the presidency, and the country.

* * * * * * * * * *

Leah and I moved from Anaheim to Los Angeles in 1986— even though I had worked at WED and Walt Disney

Imagineering in Glendale and Burbank since 1961. The drive and California freeway traffic had finally gotten to me. One day I came home and said to Leah, "I can't do this drive anymore." Her response: "I've been waiting twenty-five years for you to say that!"

As it turned out, everything moved but a unit in a storage facility, where we stuffed our son Howard's and daughter Leslie's mementos. And, of course, my treasures. When Howard and our grandson Gabriel offered to clear out that storage unit—thirty years later in December 2016—we jumped at the chance, even though it meant Howard and Gabriel coming all the way from their home in Finland to handle the job.

As I anticipated, that Anaheim storage unit was chock-full of early Disneyland and Walt Disney World materials I had written and produced—from the first hardcover book ever published about Disneyland to examples of all the key promotional materials we created to entice the park sponsors and communicate about Walt Disney World's preopening to an eager public.

I'm quite sure I have more varieties of those materials than the company's archives! And they were all in use as we prepared for the most important presentation to that point in Disney Parks and Resorts history, except for the original opening of Disneyland.

The date was April 30, 1969. There were two locations: the Parkwood Cinema in Orlando and the Ramada Inn in Ocala, about four miles east of the Magic Kingdom construction site.

When I wrote about these events for Dream It! Do It!, I gave credit to all the Disney divisions—from the Disneyland operations staff and the construction crews to corporate leaders Roy O. Disney, Card Walker, Donn Tatum, Joe Fowler, and Joe Potter. And, of course, to the Imagineers of WED Enterprises, who created all the materials for the presentation: the heroic 625-square-foot model that became the centerpiece of our presentation and photo opportunities with Disney and Florida officials, and reproduction of the key artwork of the overall project by Herb Ryman, the Monorail system by George McGinnis, and major attraction and hotel concepts by "all hands on deck"—everyone pitched in!

At the center of our presentation was the film we created, which had a life of its own—but nearly no life at all. It was my responsibility, and although my staff had created it, I was pleased enough to show it to the company's marketing chief, Card Walker, two days before we were to deliver it to Florida. That's when my biggest nightmare became reality: Card didn't like it, and I was directed to "get it right" for our presentation.

I've had long days and nights finishing projects many times over—after all, when you're dealing with thousands of pieces that have to work for the first time on an "opening day" that may have been selected three years earlier, you cross your fingers and toes a lot.

Somehow, with the support of my talented editor Jim Love, we remade the entire twenty-minute film in time for those two make-or-break previews of Walt Disney World. According to the *Orlando Star*:

Every major newspaper, wire service, television network, and magazine in the United States, as well as many foreign publications, were at today's Disney presentation on Phase One—a presentation in its way as colorful in detail as the unbelievable plans for Walt Disney World.

Or, as the *Lakeland Ledger* quoted a "sage observer" enthusing, "This is what God would have done if he'd had the money!"

For me, the thrill of watching the press and public become excited about a project still two and a half years from opening never went away—and fortunately it did not have to. In January 1970, we opened the Walt Disney World Preview Center in Lake Buena Vista. The centerpiece of the preview was the Imagineers' model and the film I had rescued. In the twenty-one months that it operated before closing on September 30, 1971, the Preview Center attracted 1,332,927 visitors.

According to John Robinett, senior vice president of economics for AECOM, an American engineering firm (which does an annual survey of theme park attendance with TEA—the Themed Entertainment Association), that more than 1.3 million attendance figure would have ranked our Preview Center "in the top ten among theme parks in the United States in 1970." And we didn't even have a single thrill ride—in fact, we had no rides at all, not even a ten-cent, coin-operated stationary car or horse outside the locale.

CHAPTER 5

"THAT'S VLADIMIR ZWORYKIN—HE INVENTED TELEVISION!"

In my experience, there were always two phases in inducing sponsors to invest large amounts of their advertising budgets to reach the public through their participation in the Disney Parks and Resorts.

First came the enticement, "the wienie," as Walt might say. And then came the knowledge and understanding about each corporation's goals and objectives.

There are few better "wienies" than experiencing a Disney park, and watching guests enjoying fun and new adventures with their families. And, of course, interacting with our cast members and seeing them carrying out the service standards that have made Disney one of the most admired companies in the world.

I keep a two-by three-inch card in my wallet. It's called "7 Guest Service Guidelines," featuring illustrations of each of the Seven Dwarfs and associated copy. Here's what it says:

These standards, carried out by our Disney park cast members, have influenced our sales efforts around the world. Several magical moments are etched in my memory.

Since its founding in 1919, the International Chamber of Commerce had always met in the capital of the host country. But for the first time, on October 2, 1978, 2,500 business executives and political leaders from around the world gathered for the organization's twenty-sixth biennial meeting—at Walt Disney World.

As President Jimmy Carter concluded his welcoming remarks in front of Cinderella Castle, it began to rain—or rather, pour. There was no way to keep those delegates dry—or was there? Suddenly, Disney cast members by the thousands, acting as hosts and hostesses, appeared from nowhere and everywhere carrying umbrellas—at least one for every one of those 2,500 delegates! It was one of those magic moments, almost as if the Fairy Godmother from *Cinderella* had emerged from the castle, waved her wand, and—"Bibbidi-Bobbidi-Boo"—everyone had something to keep the rain off their clothes. Sorry, President Carter—*umbrellas* were what everyone talked about afterwards!

On April 15, 1998, John Hench and I represented Walt Disney Parks and Resorts in celebrating the fifteenth anniversary of Tokyo Disneyland. It was a thrill to spend much of the day with Masatomo Takahashi, president and chairman of Oriental Land Company, the owner of the Tokyo Disneyland Resort (Disney is paid for all design and receives a percentage of attendance receipts, food, and merchandise sales).

Takahashi-san is considered "the father of Tokyo Disneyland"—the man whose persistence over many years finally convinced The Walt Disney Company to create the very first international Disney theme park. During its fifteenth anniversary year, Tokyo Disneyland attracted 16.7 million people—the highest attendance of any Disney park around the world that year.

But despite all the wonderful new ways to celebrate at Tokyo Disneyland—new parades, new attractions, a new live show in front of the Castle—it was the Tokyo Disney cast members who stole the show. Tokyo Disneyland's Main Street is a covered entrance avenue called World Bazaar. From the moment guests entered the park that day to join the celebration, they were greeted by every Tokyo Disneyland cast member who could spend a few minutes away from their workplace, in the costume of the attraction, each and every one greeting their guests with a warm *Yōkoso*—"Welcome" in Japanese!

Tokyo Disneyland's guests loved it—it was all about *them*, even though it was a special celebration for the Disney kingdom. Watching this sincere show of affection—*to* the guests from the cast and *from* the guests to the Tokyo Disneyland employees—John and I were overwhelmed with emotion. What a treat to be there in a land so far away from America—so far from Disneyland—watching Disney park guests enjoying the international language of joy and fun!

* * * * * * * * * *

Whenever we could expose our potential sponsors to this kind of relationship between guests and cast, of course, we did. But in truth those experiences just set the stage for the follow-up—travelling to corporate headquarters and distant ports of call to make our presentations to company leaders. No one gives you millions of dollars to create a showcase and image of their company unless you convince their corporate leaders. Maybe Pinocchio could get by "with no strings on me," but our corporate alliances dotted all the i's and crossed all the t's.

We had worked hand in hand with RCA for nine months to integrate their story of satellite communications into the guest experience at Space Mountain. It turned out to be a natural fit, leading guests seamlessly along a long corridor with views "out into space" as a prelude to the "race through space" in the attraction itself.

Now, our RCA hosts told us, there was one more step: a presentation to the company's chairman, Robert Sarnoff. It was truly a great presentation; we had nine full storyboards, each four feet by eight feet. They filled both sides of the RCA boardroom in New York City's Rockefeller Center.

Everything seemed to be going as planned, until we had completed our presentation and sat down to discuss matters with Mr. Sarnoff and his three top vice presidents. That was when the chairman wrote out a note and handed it to the closest vice president . . . who passed it on to the next VP, and the next . . . who then handed it to *me*. As I opened and read the note, I suddenly felt that the previous nine months of my life had been a fairly complete waste of time. Because the note was very succinct. It read: "Who are these people?" Meaning *me*, and my Disney associates. No one had prepped Mr. Sarnoff about why we were there—or even who we were!

It was a long flight back to Los Angeles. Fortunately, we made it back to Mr. Sarnoff's boardroom a few weeks later and convinced him that sponsoring Space Mountain was good for RCA, no matter who "these people" were.

* * * * * * * * * *

It seems as though RCA was a central focus of our efforts in the early 1970s on the road to fulfilling Disney dreams. A potential $10 million contract (equivalent to $65 million in 2017) will do that to you.

So once again we flew across the country for the meeting that would finalize RCA's agreement to sponsor the all-new, first-ever Space Mountain at the Walt Disney World Magic Kingdom—though this time we would be contending with a new vice president of public relations on their end. When we arrived for our 10:00 a.m. meeting, the door to the VP's office was closed. We were warned that he was dealing with an emergency issue; our meeting might not even take place. But we were further instructed to stay close—just in case.

Believe me, we were not going anyplace. It turned out that neither was the VP. His office was well equipped with its own bathroom, an important consideration as the day wore on. The problem, we later learned, was that an RCA television set in a New Jersey home had exploded, shattered—and tragically killed a young boy. Naturally, the VP of public relations was RCA's point person in dealing with the family, the media, and the RCA technical community.

But that wasn't quite what he was doing. Our VP contact at RCA had recently come from another company, one that manufactured automobiles, and he was not eager to deal with this kind of issue so new to him. We later learned that his solution to this problem was to lock his door, turn off the lights in his office, pretend he wasn't there—and wait for someone else at RCA to take responsibility and deal with the public and media.

And we were no exception. We never saw him that day. Ultimately, he was gone from RCA. And as it happened, on another trip, we waited outside a *new* VP's door for our patience to be rewarded with the *new* VP's signature.

During another trip to RCA's David Sarnoff Research Center in Princeton, New Jersey, we had finished a long meeting and were approaching the elevator in the building. Just as we arrived, a very short man appeared, heading for the same elevator. Suddenly our RCA hosts paused and indicated we should stop and let the "little old man" take the elevator—by himself. Puzzled, we waited until the elevator had closed and left, then asked our hosts who he was and why there was such deference paid to him.

"That," our host said, "was Vladimir Zworykin—he invented television!"

I remember reading Vladimir K. Zworykin's obituary in the *New York Times* on August 1, 1982. It confirmed our host's designation, referring to him as "the father of television," although he said he "was only one of many scientists involved." The *Times* also quoted "a birthday interview a year ago," in which Dr. Zworykin denounced the entertainment medium that television had created with one word: "Awful!"

* * * * * * * * * *

When I became Imagineering's chief spokesperson (and salesman) to corporate America in the 1970s and 1980s, I was quickly disabused of the idea that these major companies really knew how to make the best presentation of ideas and projects to their own top management. Read: "disillusioned." Here we were, making our pitch to the CEO, the CFO, the marketing VP, even board members—and shipping across the country dimensional models and original artworks worth thousands and thousands of dollars—and almost without exception, these great corporations had no facility or equipment to help us make a proper presentation.

I quickly learned that if I wanted to make an appropriate presentation, I needed to send an advance person to scout the room where we would meet the chief executive, decide what we needed to properly display our materials, and make sure the company's audiovisual staff did not screw up our sales pitch. More often than not, that meant bringing or purchasing our own lights, figuring out how to hang artwork on walls you could not hammer a nail into, and overcoming automatically triggered systems like lighting whenever a venue like a board of directors room was used. No kidding—I'm talking about the Exxons and GEs and MetLifes of American industry, the corporate giants in their fields.

There was one special venue, however, that not only supplied everything we needed, but was built and operated to make sure its presentations (and those from visitors) showcased the company's products in the most optimal ways. That venue was the General Motors Design Center in Warren, Michigan. Want your new car to shine like a jewel, to be lit and "perform" like a Hollywood star? You could do it with all the glitz and glamour of a 1960s Detroit auto show right there in the GM Design Dome.

Part of the famous GM Technical Center, opened in the mid-1950s, the Design Dome was created by Eero Saarinen, the Finnish architect who would go on to design some of mid-century America's best-known icons, including the TWA terminal at JFK airport in New York City (1962) and the Gateway Arch in St. Louis (1965).

The brainchild of Harley Earl, the pioneering GM design chief who created the Motorama shows of the 1950s and 1960s, Saarinen's Design Dome was called "the holy place for our designers" by one of GM's head designers, Ed Welburn. Since this was where the GM corporate moguls approved the final design of a new vehicle, it was said that "virtually every vehicle GM has made since the 1956 model year cleared the last hurdle before production in the Design Dome." Some rhapsodized its importance this way: "It's where today meets tomorrow."

Now it was our turn to get over that last hurdle and bring GM into our world of Epcot. For perhaps the first time since that Walt Disney presentation to "that other automobile company, Ford," we were faced with the challenge of convincing two different audiences that they should trust in us: the corporate hierarchy and their venerated design leadership.

GM's design staff knew how to show off their vehicles. Once when John Hench and I visited the Design Dome, John expressed his admiration for the Corvette Stingray to Bill Mitchell, GM's executive design chief. The very next morning, when we arrived for another meeting, Mitchell had brought out for our inspection one of every model of the Corvette that had *ever* been produced. Guess who had designed the original? Bill Mitchell was truly proud of his achievement.

We had to decide exactly how we were going to fill the Saarinen dome—all 39,500 square feet of it.

We had been invited late in 1977 to make a presentation for sponsorship in Epcot by Roger Smith, then executive vice president, and later GM's chairman and CEO from 1981 to 1990. Roger's role in 1977 included chairing the company's "Scenario 2000 Advisory Committee"—which was responsible for setting the course for GM's future. For GM, the question was this: Could Epcot play a role in that future? For Disney, the question was this: Could GM sign on the dotted line as *the first major corporation* to sponsor an Epcot pavilion . . . and in so doing, in a real sense, make the project feasible?

Obviously, the stakes were high for both parties. From Disney's perspective, this was an all-or-nothing moment.

Keeping in mind those two audiences—Roger Smith and his executive committee, and the professional design staff of the GM Design Dome—we decided to pull out all the stops. First, we arranged to gather every key element of the project that would "sell" our ideas and ship them to Warren, Michigan. What we sent was not just illustrations and models for a proposed "Transportation Pavilion"—but renderings for *every* pavilion we were developing in Future World and the World Showcase. That meant artworks, storyboards, plans, pavilion models, even engineering information about buildings and land conditions for the site plan.

Then we made the really big decision: we hired John DeCuir to fill those 39,500 square feet of the Design Dome with a presentation that would "knock the socks off" even Bill Mitchell and his design staff.

Imagineering had worked with John DeCuir before. He was one of Hollywood's premier art directors and production designers, nominated for eleven Academy Awards and a recipient of three—for *The King and I* (1956), *Cleopatra* (1963), and *Hello, Dolly!* (1969). John DeCuir had answered Dick Irvine's call in 1970 and directed an amazing team of artists in creating the Hall of Presidents show for Liberty Square in the Magic Kingdom.

You know you have made the right call when your audience gasps when they walk into a familiar place and sees it "all new." Sure enough, John DeCuir created a scene worthy of a good gasp—he had turned GM's auto showplace into Disney's vision of Epcot.

The pitch was a smashing success, so much so that Jack Lindquist and I were left behind, along with all the models and artwork, to show them to GM president Pete Estes early the following morning. Between 7:00 and 9:00 the next day we did indeed meet and present our pitch to Estes and several other GM leaders. And by December 31, 1977, General Motors had become the first major Epcot corporate sponsor.

By the way, that sponsorship, now focused on the Chevrolet division of GM, continues, featuring the thrilling Test Track attraction in the very same spot.

The Hollywood connection worked so well with GM that we tried it again with Exxon and art director Jack Martin Smith. He had "only" been nominated for nine Academy Awards, and had shared in three—with John DeCuir for *Cleopatra* and *Hello, Dolly!*, and with his 20th Century Fox colleagues for *Fantastic Voyage*.

We had encouraged a "race" between GM and Exxon to see which would sign to become Epcot's first pavilion sponsor. With GM confirmed, we focused on Exxon, scheduling a presentation early in 1978 in New York City to Chairman Clifton Garvin.

To dramatize our story about energy—and to create a family-friendly show—we began our ride-through story with the period in Earth's history when many of our fossil fuels were formed. That gave us an opportunity to create a drama with huge dinosaurs roaming the land.

Imagine my shock when, at the key moment of our presentation, Jack Smith suddenly dropped to one knee and spoke directly to the chairman: "Mr. Garvin," he enthused, focusing on the dinosaurs, "these are the Marilyn Monroes of your pavilion."

I have seldom lost the power of speech in a presentation . . . but on this occasion, I was totally flabbergasted and unable to utter a word. Somehow, we recovered and made the sale. Exxon became the second major pavilion sponsor in Epcot. I shall always be indebted to Mr. Garvin for his courtesy. I suspect he had no trouble distinguishing those terrestrial vertebrates from the bipedal primates of Ms. Monroe's time.

* * * * * * * * * *

Just a word or two more about some of the CEOs we presented to over the years, with emphasis on Walt Disney World and Epcot. I've mentioned two of my favorites (Roger Smith of GM and Cliff Garvin of Exxon) and two of my biggest challenges (Robert Sarnoff and Jack Welch). Following are capsule experiences with three more chief executives illustrating that CEOs, like the companies they lead, come in a wide variety of personalities.

If you twisted my arm and forced me to name my favorite of the CEOs we worked with at other companies, it would be **William O. Beers.** He was chairman and CEO of Kraft from 1972 to 1979; during his term, Kraft became the largest processor of manufactured and processed foods in the world.

Mr. Beers had started his career at Kraft as an assistant cheese maker in Wisconsin. In reading about his background, I learned that he had spent two years holding three-day meetings at his Wisconsin farm with two hundred executives, taking them in groups of twenty, to resolve a gap between top and middle management. That helped explain my experience with Bill Beers.

During a presentation to Kraft of our concepts for The Land in a conference room at our offices in Glendale, Mr. Beers received a telephone call, which he took in my nearby office.

As we walked back to the conference room, he stopped for a moment and confided in me: "Marty, each of those nine people in that conference room runs a key division of Kraft, Inc.—and they never get together to address the challenges we have. That's why I want to be part of Epcot: it gives each of them a chance to work together on a high-profile project, and focus on communicating our company's leadership in the food business!"

Mr. Beers moved to Arizona when he retired in 1983. We continued to correspond until his passing in 1992 at age seventy-seven.

"No one ever achieved greatness by playing it safe" is an aptly attributed quote from **Harry J. Gray**. His career makes it clear that Harry lived his corporate life that way.

Harry Gray was chairman and CEO of United Technologies Corp. (UTC) from 1974 to 1986. Harry built the company beginning as president of United Aircraft (manufacturers of Pratt & Whitney jet engines) and by later acquiring Otis Elevator Company, Carrier (maker of heating and air conditioning equipment), and other companies.

Our Disney chairman, Card Walker, met Mr. Gray on a golf outing in Hawaii in the early 1980s, and in 1986, we opened The Living Seas pavilion in Epcot with United Technologies as the corporate sponsor.

Harry Gray was the kind of CEO about whom you could easily say, "It's my way or the highway" . . . in other words, *his way*, of course. Yet we really enjoyed the challenge of creating The Living Seas with Harry and his team. One reason was we knew they wanted the pavilion to work for UTC, and they paid close attention to *everything* we developed. Every month or so, those Pratt & Whitney engines brought

Harry and his executive staff to Glendale to review our progress and provide input.

I developed a good rapport with **Ray D'Argenio**, UTC's senior public relations executive. In a meeting in Hartford, Connecticut—UTC's headquarters—I saw Ray making a drawing; after the meeting, I asked for an explanation, and he quickly wrote names under his sketch:

WED   **Harry**

It was clearly a lesson in who's the boss. There was no question with Harry Gray, as we were to find out over and over again. Among other things, Harry Gray provided one of my favorite stories about working with corporate clients in the development of Epcot.

The CEO of United Technologies let it be known that he wanted the exterior walls of The Living Seas pavilion to be painted a bright white. John Hench, one of the most knowledgeable designers in the world on the theory and effect of color, visually and emotionally, let Mr. Gray know that he did not use a bright white in Florida because the reflection of the sun could be blinding to approaching guests. Harry asked for a demonstration.

While the pavilion was under construction, we erected temporary walls six feet high around the front of the building. On a bright, sunny afternoon, John Hench lined up the painters and, when Harry and Helen Gray arrived, established the parameters of the discussion. "Mr. Gray," John said, "I use thirty-four shades of white in our parks. Which one would you like to see?"

While Harry pondered his response, Helen Gray gripped my arm and drew me aside. "Marty, why are you asking Harry about color?" she asked. "I pick out his ties every morning because he's color-blind!"

John Joseph Creedon is another CEO I continued to interface with long after he retired as the head of MetLife. I really don't know why, except we somehow hit it off from the beginning of our relationship. Maybe it was *his* relationship with John Tishman; they were partners in hotels, and John Tishman and I developed a friendship during the building of Epcot, for which Tishman Construction served as the general contractor.

Disney had an auspicious beginning with Mr. Creedon: MetLife had agreed to finance a hotel, which the Tishman organization would operate, on the Walt Disney World property. When the arrangement fell into dispute, the Tishman–MetLife partnership threatened to sue Disney.

How the hotel conflict was resolved is relevant to this story only in the fact that we were anxious to include a pavilion in Epcot related to life and health. Mr. Creedon became intrigued, and the Wonders of Life pavilion, opened in 1989, was the result. It included some of the most engaging attractions in Epcot: *The Making of Me*, a film about birth starring Martin Short; Cranium Command, where audiences were immersed in a three-dimensional show illustrating how a thirteen-year-old boy's brain functioned; Body Wars, a motion-simulator ride inspired, in many ways, by the film *Fantastic Voyage*; and an interactive area including Goofy About Health, Fitness Fairgrounds, Coach's Corner, and other fun experiences.

Mr. Creedon began his MetLife career in 1942. Later he earned his law degree, became president of MetLife in 1980, served as president and CEO from 1983 to 1989, and continued as a member of the corporation's advisory council until 2006.

But he must have had an instinct for how the world of entertainment could open doors for MetLife. In 1985, MetLife signed an agreement with *Peanuts* cartoon creator Charles Shulz to use Snoopy, Charlie Brown, Lucy, and other characters—an obvious attempt to make an insurance company more friendly and approachable. This was a triumph for John Creedon; for the next thirty-one years those characters became the key to MetLife's marketing and sales material . . . and the inspiration for the famous Snoopy blimp soaring overhead at sports events, parades, and so many special occasions.

Unfortunately, MetLife did not renew its contract and Wonders of Life was closed at Epcot in 2007.

I've always felt very lucky to have learned from all those CEOs, not to mention the six men I had the privilege to serve under at The Walt Disney Company: Roy O. Disney, Donn Tatum, Card Walker, Ron Miller, Michael Eisner, and Bob Iger.

And Walt Disney? Perhaps he was too wise to become CEO. As he wrote in an essay called "Take a Chance:"

> Now I'm a grandfather and have a good many gray hairs and what a lot of people would call common sense. But if I'm no longer young in age, I hope I stay young enough in spirit never to fear failure—young enough still to take a chance and march in the parade.

CHAPTER 6

THE FUTURIST WHO DIDN'T FLY (OR DRIVE) AND OTHER LEGENDS

This is a tale about travel, so let's start with this: it's true that science fiction writer and futurist Ray Bradbury did not fly or drive!

Yes, this is *that* Ray Bradbury—the one who wrote *The Martian Chronicles* (1950), *The Illustrated Man* (1951), *Fahrenheit 451* (1953), and a total of twenty-seven novels and six hundred short stories. His flights of fantasy and visual imagination led President Barack Obama to issue this statement when Ray passed away at age ninety-one in 2012:

> *For many Americans, the news of Ray Bradbury's death immediately brought to mind images from his work imprinted on our minds, often from a young age. His gift for storytelling reshaped our culture and expanded our world. But Ray understood that our imaginations could be used as a tool for better*

understanding, an expression of our most cherished values. There is no doubt that Ray will continue to inspire many more generations with his writing.

When I noted the dates Ray Bradbury's best-known stories were published, I was reminded of the impact Ray had on me as a young reader—and writer. In 1950 and 1951, I was still in high school; by 1953, I was a sophomore at UCLA, majoring in political science and writing for the *Daily Bruin* student newspaper, where I would soon serve as editor in chief.

Is it any surprise that Imagineering would reach out to Ray Bradbury when we began to develop the story concept for our theme show in Epcot Center—the 180-foot-high geodesic sphere that dominates the park's entrance? In Spaceship Earth, our goal was to tell a story of how humankind evolved through the centuries in parallel to our ability to communicate. As President Obama wrote, "Ray understood that our imaginations could be used as a tool for better understanding."

One trait of Ray Bradbury's that I admired was his discipline. The first thing he did every day at his home in the Cheviot Hills area of Los Angeles was sit down at his typewriter and *write something*. "Just type any old thing that comes into your head," he advised would-be writers. "You don't know what's in your head until you test it."

Long after our days working with Ray on Epcot, Imagineering designer Tim Delaney suggested we visit Ray at his home in Cheviot Hills. Ray had admired Tim's illustrations, and they had become friends. By then, Ray had suffered a stroke, affecting his speech and motor skills. But in his home environment, surrounded by copies of his books, magazine stories, and the artifacts he loved, Ray was still the king of his kingdom.

I was reminded of the time Bradbury asked Walt Disney to run for mayor of Los Angeles: "Ray," Walt responded, "why should I run for mayor when I'm already king of Disneyland?"

Tim Delaney summed up our affection for—and our working relationship with—Ray Bradbury in a note to me:

One of the greatest experiences of my life was my relationship with Ray Bradbury, the great fantasy writer. Over the course of twenty-five years, at an interval of every 6 to 8 weeks, I visited Ray in his home, where we talked about everything "under the sun." I kept my visits with Ray to about an hour, always mindful of this great opportunity and his precious time. In those hours we toured the universe of ideas, creativity, people, life, and the Walt Disney Company.

Ray's love of the Walt Disney Company started with Steamboat Willie and "exploded" when he first saw Fantasia. Ray's stories on Fantasia focused on two subjects—that he saw the film over a hundred times and that any friend of his who didn't share his love of this film was no longer a friend.

The day that Ray met Walt Disney was an epic event for him. While at the Bullock's Wilshire department store at Christmas time, Ray saw a man carrying a large stack of presents and quickly recognized Walt. He walked up to Walt, introduced himself, and Walt immediately asked Ray to come to the Disney Studio for lunch the next day.

That lunch was a powerful moment in Ray's life. Walt continued talking with Ray long after the hour was over, much to the unhappiness of Walt's secretary, who had to reschedule Walt's afternoon appointments. At the end of the lunch Walt asked Ray what he wanted. Ray's answer: "Open the vaults" to allow him to go into the Archives and take several animation cels from his favorite movies, Snow White being the most prominent. Ray's love of Disney animation was rewarded and he treasured his collection his entire life.

Ray Bradbury always considered himself a city planner. He met with the Los Angeles City Council on several occasions to push for Walt's monorail as a Southern California transit solution. This is the reason he loved being at Walt Disney Imagineering. The other reason was his love of the Imagineers, especially John Hench, Marty Sklar, Marc Davis, and any of the original studio animation team that worked at WDI. Ray's description of the Imagineers as the Renaissance People is well chronicled.

There was no more perfect project for Ray than Epcot. The opportunity to work on Walt Disney's City of Tomorrow was a dream come true for Ray. He always saw himself as one of the original "dreamers and doers." Ray's work on Spaceship Earth provided a foundation for all of Epcot. His eternal positive and optimistic energy can be felt throughout the entire park.

In 1985, I asked Ray to join my Discoveryland team for some brainstorming on ideas for a land at

Disneyland Paris that was to be dedicated to the great visionaries of Europe—Jules Verne, H.G. Wells, Leonardo da Vinci. My goal was to create a unique Tomorrowland that was a collection of futures and Ray was the man I needed. It was a pleasure to work with Ray in that his ideas were non-stop, except of course when he would stop to run over to any available typewriter to write and polish his ideas in his poetic style. Those were great and memorable times, ones that I will cherish forever.

Toward the end of his life, my visits to Ray changed. We still reminisced about Disney, his numerous visits to Disneyland, which included commandeering a Jungle Cruise boat with the great actor Charles Laughton, who took on the role of Captain Bligh much to Ray's delight, and his days working on Epcot. The big change, however, was his desire for me to read to him, which I did.

I read his stories to him. I believe he wanted to visit those adventures one more time. It made him happy and I am glad I was there.

* * * * * * * * *

I had the opportunity on three different occasions to join Ray Bradbury for special interview programs. One was at the national convention of Science and Technology Centers meeting in Los Angeles; the session was moderated by film critic, author, and historian Leonard Maltin. The other two programs were in support of our friend Waynn Pearson, the ingenious city librarian who created "the library of tomorrow" in 2002—the Cerritos Millennium Library in Southern California.

Inspired by Disneyland itself, and motivated by the best-selling book *The Experience Economy* by Joe Pine, Waynn Pearson was able to create placemaking that rivaled an attraction in the theme park world. It was so attractive from a design point of view that it even won an award from the Themed Entertainment Association in 2003 for Outstanding Achievement. Beyond books and the traditional library services, the children's area included a saltwater aquarium, an ocean lighthouse, a rain forest, and a Tyrannosaurus rex fossil replica. The library also has a "Main Street," an art deco reading room, and two hundred computer workstations—a magnet for the students at the high school directly across the street.

Ray Bradbury loved the place—his love of libraries never diminished. So the Bradbury–Sklar team did two fundraising events: public question and answer sessions in 2007 that were popular with fans of the Cerritos Library. It was all I could do to keep up with the twists and turns and leaps and bounds and changes of direction of Ray's mind and interests. I was exhausted just trying to stay on the same page, and in the same story, with that incredible man of verbal illustrations.

But it was Spaceship Earth, and Epcot itself, that truly motivated Bradbury in his working relationship with our Imagineering team. And we were motivated by him! In a Disney tribute on Ray's death, I recounted the formal role he played and how he motivated me personally:

Ray did a story treatment that became the framework
for the communication theme of Spaceship Earth
at Epcot—and the first draft of his "summary" ran

*14 pages! Of course, he was a storyteller; it was
our job to turn his prose and metaphors into a ride
experience. I will always treasure Ray's philosophy
of what he called "optimal behaviorism: Make sure
when you wake up in the morning that you know
you accomplished everything you possibly could the
previous day. And then do it again!"*

I was far from alone in being inspired by Ray Bradbury.
He was "prolific and deeply influential . . . as an unmatched
author of science fiction and fantasy," as the Pulitzer cita-
tion he received in 2007 expressed it. John Hench and I,
recognizing the value of Ray's power to inspire, asked him
to speak to an assembly of all the Imagineers. Here is what
he said:

*John and Marty told me I was supposed to come up
here and explain you to yourselves . . . and to tell you
what you are and what I am and what I'm doing here.
I'm here because I want to be here. There are a lot of
places in the world I could be, but I've been coming
through WED and going to Disneyland for many years
now and I like what I see.*

*A wonderful thing happened to me in 1954 . . .
I went to Italy for the first time ever. I travelled
through Rome and Florence and Venice. I saw the
works of Fra Angelico and I came home inundated
with the Renaissance. By a wonderful coincidence,
a few months later, I came out to the Disney Studio
and wandered through and saw the sketches and the
drawings and the paintings for "Sleeping Beauty."*

I said, "My God . . . This is fantastic, that I'm seeing work here commensurate with many of the things that I saw in Renaissance Italy when I visited there for the first time . . ."

And so, really, what you are is Renaissance People. If ever there was a Renaissance organization, this is it. You haven't peaked yet, but you're peaking, and sometime in the next twenty years when you peak completely, the whole world's going to be looking at you.

So, we start with "Sleeping Beauty" and we go on to another thing. For the first time in 1969 I was in London and I went through the Victoria and Albert Museum. Now, I don't know how many of you have gone through that place . . . it sounds awfully stuffy, doesn't it, when you say "Victoria and Albert Museum"? But what you're talking about is the true Victoria, which is a sense of adventure, excitement, curiosity . . . going out into the world and borrowing, stealing from all the arts . . . all the cultures . . . all the ideas of time.

Victoria was an incredible woman . . . she sent her explorers out, she sent her artists out, and they went down to Italy and took casts of Hadrian's Column and all the great statues. They imported the damn stuff by ship around the Rock and up to England, and it took years for each of these projects to come about. So I wandered through the Victoria and Albert Museum and I come here, and I have the same experience . . . of people who have been out in the world, and have seen and tasted and touched and loved and you've *brought it all back, and it's here. And that's very important to say. . . .*

Your contributions, then, are of two of the greatest periods in history. When you think of the Renaissance and what went on there, and you think of the Victorians, who were just as incredible in their own way—and changed the world forever . . . you're doing the same thing here. . . .

It's a big project. But of all the groups in the world, while everyone else is busy talking, you're doing the stuff that's really going to count.

* * * * * * * * * *

The opening of EPCOT Center on October 1, 1982, was a major international event, covered by news media from around the world and celebrated by the dual Concorde landings. All of our core crew of Imagineers, as well as consultants, celebrities, and influential people from relevant fields, were invited to participate in the festivities. Of course, we wanted Ray, who was so instrumental in framing the central theme of the project, to attend. There was just one problem: the renowned futurist, whose works had taken us on flights of fantasy to Mars, did not drive and would not fly! In Los Angeles, the city of cars, where Ray had lobbied for a monorail transit system, Ray travelled by bicycle. For travel outside of Los Angeles, Ray relied on trains. It turned out he had taken several trains that routed him to New Orleans for a speaking engagement several days before the opening. John Hench was able to convince Ray to join us in Florida after his speech—but how to get him there? Ray solved the problem: he hired a driver who took him the nine hours and 640 highway miles from New Orleans, Louisiana, to Orlando, Florida.

It was great to have Ray with us to tell the media things like this:

What Disney is doing is showing the world that there are alternative ways to do things that can make us all happy. If we can borrow some of the concepts of Disneyland and Disney World and EPCOT, then indeed the world can be a better place.

Now the ceremonies were over, and one issue remained related to Ray Bradbury: how to get the man who did not fly back to Los Angeles from Orlando? Once again, it was John Hench who came to the rescue: he talked and talked—probably read Ray's palm, too—and finally convinced Ray Bradbury to take *his first ever airplane flight*, accompanying John on his return to Los Angeles.

Years later, the author of *The Martian Chronicles* and so many other flights of fantasy revealed how he worked up the nerve to take his first airplane ride. "I had a bit to drink," he admitted, science factually!

In retrospect, I consider that achievement—convincing Ray Bradbury to see the stars in the night sky from aboard an airplane—to be one of the most remarkable achievements in John Hench's career.

* * * * * * * * * *

Our good fortune as Imagineers has been the opportunity to work with some of the greatest talents in our industry. In my time, one of the most significant relationships we enjoyed was with George Lucas, creator of the Star Wars and Indiana

Jones films—two of the movie industry's all-time most loved and successful franchises.

Long before Disney, under the leadership of Bob Iger, acquired George Lucas's company in 2012, Imagineering built a solid working relationship with George Lucas. I asked Tom Fitzgerald, Imagineering's senior creative executive and the point person in our dealings with Lucas, to write about that creative relationship.

In the early 1980s, we invited George Lucas to visit our Imagineering headquarters in Southern California, to discuss whether we might work together on projects. We were, like the rest of the world, huge fans of George's Star Wars *and* Raiders of the Lost Ark *films. And George, we discovered, was a huge fan of Disneyland, having visited the park at its opening back in 1955.*

As part of his tour of our WED (now Walt Disney Imagineering—WDI) facility, George saw various models and artwork for projects under consideration. One that immediately caught his attention was a storyboard outlining how a new motion-base simulator would allow guests to experience lifelike sensations as never before. George sparked to this as an ideal ride platform for a Star Wars *adventure.*

Before long Tony Baxter and I were headed to London to test-ride the new simulator system. The simulators had been designed by a company that built flight simulators for airline pilots, but we instantly saw the potential for a Star Wars *space adventure and returned home to brainstorm potential story lines.*

Of the various ideas we later presented to George, he picked the "Space Tour Company" concept as the best fit for Disneyland. As the show developed, George championed the idea of combining comedy with a thrill ride, and the now-classic story line "where something goes horribly wrong" and we get pulled into a heroic adventure. He also encouraged us to capitalize on ideas that would read quickly in our short-story medium, saying, "Don't avoid the clichés. They're clichés because they work!"

Throughout production, George would review film dailies with ILM (Industrial Light & Magic, the originators of the Star Wars visual effects magic) and check in on programming of the motion base at Imagineering. George was on hand to cut the ribbon—with a lightsaber, of course—at Disneyland in early 1987, and at other Disney park locations around the world.

When George began work on the prequel Star Wars films (Episodes I–III) we felt it was time to refresh the attraction and developed a branching story line to allow us to incorporate as many adventures as possible. During the production, George worked with us intimately on the 3-D sequences, helping guide the action and impact of every moment. He pushed for deeper audience interaction with the story line, which resulted in the Rebel Spy gag (where an image of an audience member appears on the screens in the cabin as part of the show).

George's knowledge and love for both Star Wars and Disneyland made him the ultimate partner for

*the Star Tours (and later Indiana Jones) attractions.
The Force was strong with this relationship, and the
results continue to entertain millions of Disney guests
around the world!*

* * * * * * * * * *

As I reflected on the success and enjoyment our teams at
Walt Disney Imagineering had with Ray Bradbury, George
Lucas, ocean explorer Bob Ballard, astronauts—including
Mercury 7 "original" Gordon Cooper—and so many more,
I wanted to know how our friends in the themed entertainment industry thought about their experiences with what
we call "outside talent"—meaning experts in their fields
who are not members of their in-house company teams. So
I asked a few of my friends who are leaders in the Themed
Entertainment Association, an organization of more than
1,300 companies and individuals who create attractions,
exhibits, and shows for themed environments (not just the
parks, but museums, water parks, zoos, restaurants, and
other "compelling places and experiences"). What follow
are several of the responses that I received.

Phil Hettema is president and creative executive of the
Hettema Group. His "karma" in the park business includes
his birth year (1955), the same year Disneyland opened.
As a student at California State University, Long Beach, he
began his career in parade design and costume development at Walt Disney's Anaheim park. But it was as a producer and director at Universal Creative that Phil grew into
a major force in the industry, contributing to such shows
as Back to the Future: The Ride; The Amazing Adventures
of Spider-Man; Backdraft; Jurassic Park: The Ride; and the

Islands of Adventure park in Florida. He formed the Hettema Group in 2002 and has created such signature projects as the film *Beyond All Boundaries* for the National World War II Museum in New Orleans, and the One World Observatory in New York City—part of the remarkable memorial to those who perished in the 9/11 attack on the World Trade Center.* Here's Phil:

I have headed my own firm for over a decade, and in that time we've provided consulting services to dozens of clients, and we've also engaged numerous consultant firms and dozens of talented individual consultants to fill out our project teams.

Working with creative talent is one of the true joys of our industry. Put the right talent together in a productive situation and it's astounding what can be accomplished. But it takes both diplomacy and good management skills to make it all work. Creative individuals are unique personalities who require respect and validation. Talented individuals can also occasionally be sensitive, or even temperamental, and sometimes need a little "special handling." On the other hand, clients are often guilty of treating consultant talent as a commodity.

Every individual or studio-for-hire has their own particular strengths, and "casting" the right skill set for any task can make a big difference. Collaborating with the right talent can take a project to a much higher

*Editor's note: In 2018 Phil received the Buzz Price Thea Award—Recognizing a Lifetime of Distinguished Achievements. Phil is also the president of the Board of Directors of Ryman Arts.

level, but casting a project wrong can slow the whole process down. No individual or studio is right for every project. The better the client understands the capabilities they're hiring, the better the match can be.

No matter which "side of the fence" you find yourself on, experience tells me that talent collaboration is most successful when the work results in a win-win scenario. The work can be incredibly productive and satisfying, or it can become incredibly stressful and painful on both sides. Like so much in life, the client/consultant partnership is a relationship, and it can have all the ups and downs the word implies.

A few tips for success . . .

- Respect and acknowledge the talent of the consultant.
- Communicate your expectations clearly.
- Provide consistent project feedback and clear direction.
- Remember you are probably not this consultant's only client. When you create a great work relationship, the consultant will want to help solve your problems.
- Take a moment to put yourself in the consultant's shoes.

Some of the best collaborations I've ever enjoyed have been with the incredible freelance individuals in our industry. If both sides communicate well and follow the rules above, and also know they can trust each other, together they can stretch the creative possibilities of a project and achieve amazing things!

* * * * * * * * * *

Now let's look at this relationship from the expert consultant side.

Mark Fuller is the CEO and chief creative talent of WET, a design firm specializing in water features. I loved working with Mark when he created the iconic Leapfrog Fountains at the Imagination pavilion in Epcot (using a laminar flow technology that he had invented) and the dramatic Fountain of Nations. Since forming his own company, WET Design, in 1983, Mark has led his organization in creating over two hundred fountains and water features in twenty countries around the world, using water, fire, ice, fog, and lighting. Perhaps his signature works are the Fountains of Bellagio in Las Vegas and the world's largest performing fountain, the Dubai Fountain in the United Arab Emirates. Among his "trophies" are the Lifetime Achievement Award from the Themed Entertainment Association, and recognition as a "notable alumnus" from the University of Utah, where he received a degree in civil and environmental engineering. The *New Yorker* magazine called him "the closest thing the world has to a fountain genius."

Here's how Mark Fuller approaches the "ask" by his clients for something new and wonderful:

I tell my team that the information we want to extract from clients is similar to what doctors extract from patients. "Hey doc, my neighbor takes these incredible pills. They're bright pink and make her feel great! Can I have some?" Depending on the doctor's bedside manner, the replies range from "Not a chance!" to "Well, no, but let's discuss what you need."

Clients new to WET often believe in this miracle pill approach to attracting and entertaining people. They come to us saying, "I love the Bellagio fountain! I want the same thing for my project." (Usually followed by "only smaller and cheaper.") But it quickly becomes apparent that their project is not a casino, but rather a civic park, or a shopping center, or a children's hospital, none of which would benefit from a fountain created specifically for the Bellagio casino in Las Vegas. What they're looking to achieve requires its own dedicated consideration and ideation. So even if we did copy ourselves (which we don't), the same pill simply doesn't work for everyone.

And it doesn't take long to figure that out. Let's say the civic park client wants a memorial to honor a local philanthropist or the hospital wants to captivate little kids while their parents await the discharge of Aunt Lucy or the shopping center that's been there forever is now suffering since the cool new mall opened three blocks away. These are all symptoms that require completely different prescriptions and, in these cases, we are the doctors who have to identify the symptoms and design remedies for each client. For the shopping center, we determine that the client wants to delight their visitors, keep them happy and shopping for as long as possible, specifically attract a hip young crowd, and pivot from all the clichés of a typical mall. Well, we know just how to do that. And away we go. . . .

Once we have a firm understanding of the client's needs, we create a solution specific to them, to their

For the 116th annual Tournament of Roses Parade, Marty and his fellow judges spent three days evaluating the floats for their design, floral use, and theme.

Leah was by Marty's side when he was honored with the Themed Entertainment Association's Thea Lifetime Achievement Award in 1995.

Ray Bradbury and Jack Lindquist shared some laughs with Marty and the audience at the Thea Awards ceremony in 1995.

Celebrations

Three men in hats—Disney Legends Marty, landscape designer Bill Evans, and John Hench—share a moment at the tenth anniversary of Walt Disney World's opening.

Marty surprised everyone when he suddenly appeared onstage with emcee Neil Patrick Harris and the Dapper Dans to receive the Diane Disney Miller Lifetime Achievement Award from The Walt Disney Family Museum in 2016.

Nothing says "celebration" like a balloon release! This celebration is for Tokyo Disneyland's fifth anniversary.

In a long-standing family tradition, Marty took this 2017 photo of the grandchildren—left to right, Gabriel, Jacob, Hannah, and Rachel—in Disneyland's Hub, with the statue of Walt and Mickey and Sleeping Beauty Castle in the background.

The Sklar family travelled to Tokyo Disney Resort in 2009. Left to right, Howard, Rachel, Leah, Leslie, Jacob, Gabriel, Marty, Hannah, and Katriina.

This annual photo of the grandchildren in front of the statue of Walt and Mickey was taken at Disneyland Paris. Left to right: Jacob, Gabriel, Rachel, and Hannah.

Marty and Leah's grandchildren— Jacob, Rachel, Gabriel, and Hannah—pose at an atelier in Paris for a spirited take on their yearly studio photo portrait.

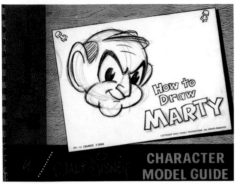

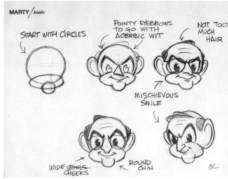

In celebration of Marty's fiftieth anniversary with Disney, Imagineer Chris Runco captured Marty's evolving style in his amusing *How to Draw Marty* guide.

Sam McKim, one of Disneyland's earliest illustrators and a Disney Legend, put a Western spin on his colorful tribute to Marty's then forty years with Disney.

Joe Rohde, creative lead on Walt Disney World's Animal Kingdom, illustrated some animals not seen at the park in this celebration of Marty's fortieth anniversary with The Walt Disney Company.

Kevin Rafferty hearkened back to Marty's early days as editor of *The Disneyland News* to mark Marty's fiftieth anniversary with the company. And here's Marty at his very first job for Disney, examining an edition of *The Disneyland News* hot off the presses.

Tributes

Herbert Ryman liked to imagine Marty as a "Sklargoyle," as illustrated here in his response to Marty's request for recommendations of places to see and things to do in Europe.

For Marty's fiftieth anniversary, Frank Armitage offered two portraits of Marty, who couldn't resist joking that his left side was his best.

Sometimes words aren't necessary: graphic designer, Ryman board member, and friend Wayne Hunt sent this tender condolence "letter" to Leah memorializing Marty's many passions.

The entrance to the Walt Disney World property, seen here in 1968, with Marty casually leaning against a post, gave no hint to the magic that would be created in a few short years.

Disney Legend Mary Blair strikes a pose with her mural prior to its installation in the Contemporary Resort. The image reveals the grand scale of the colorful and playful mural that is the centerpiece of the hotel.

A Contemporary Resort guest room slides into place in the modular construction project uniting Disney and U.S. Steel.

Marty captured this moment of the Monorail gliding out of the Contemporary Resort, vindicating John Hench's refusal to accept a redesign eliminating the transportation feature.

Dear Walt

The Orange Bird, originally created by Robert Moore as the "spokesbird" for Florida Orange Commission in return for their attractions sponsorship, has recently come out of retirement at Tokyo Disneyland and in vintage Walt Disney World merchandise.

Robert Moore and Paul Wenzel designed the 1968 postage stamp featuring Walt Disney surrounded by an international cast of children holding hands.

Walt Disney stands behind the model for the original "it's a small world," while Mary Blair's whimsical designs for the attraction are crafted into three-dimensional figures.

Among the treasures retrieved from an Anaheim storage unit was this letter to the late Walt Disney, written in 1967 by Marty—in felt-tip pen on six pages from his pocket notebook and seen here for the first time. Opposite is the full letter.

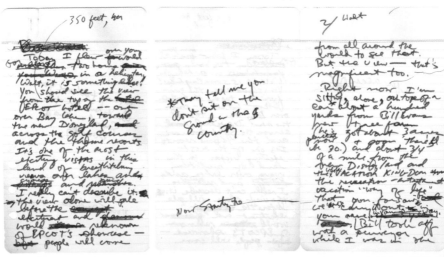

Sunday, Nov. 5 – 67 In Disney World

Dear Walt –

Today I flew over your World for about 2 hours, in a helicopter. Walt, words are always tough enough to come by, but this is really something else! You should see the view from 350 feet—the top of the EPCOT Hotel—the view out over Bay Lake, toward the new Disneyland, across the golf courses and the theme resorts. It's one of the most exciting vistas in this land of breathtaking views over lakes and cypress and pines and oak.

I really can't describe it, Walt. I know the view alone will pale before the excitement and world stature of EPCOT's showplace and showcase for American free enterprise—people will come from everywhere in the world to see that. But the view alone—that's magnificent too.

Right now, I'm sitting, alone, on top of a car (they tell me you don't dare sit on the ground in this country)—about 100 yards from Bill Evans' new tree farm (he's got about three acres planted now and soon there'll be 30), and about ¾ of a mile from the new Disneyland and the whole "Vacation Kingdom." Except for its location (a little farther north and east than you foresaw because of the swamp), this is the recreation-entertainment-vacation "way of life" that you planned. Now, we're starting to carry it out in your name, and, we all hope and pray, in your way.

Bill Evans took off with a surveyor while I was top side in the chopper, looking over a cameraman's shoulder. So I'm just sitting here on top of an Avis on a gorgeous, clear, sunny, Sunday afternoon in November. And just sitting here, seeing some of the cleared land, watching a few trucks roll by, and thinking back to what I have just seen from the air, I marvel at the strength and logic of it all. We flew up from the intersection of I-4 and 530, and everything just seemed to fall right into place. I guess that shouldn't have surprised me. But I hadn't, as you did, lived and died with this plan . . . lived with it in planning it, and died with it as you traced it over and over again on your hospital room ceiling. I'm told these were your last thoughts, and now I can understand why you would have chosen this particular thought as your last—over Mickey or Snow White or Mary Poppins or Cal Arts—yes, even Disneyland.

I've heard that every planner and architect who has seen it says this is THE master plan. But you really have to see it—drive it and fly it and touch it—to really feel Disney World as you must have. Please count me in.

Given 3 or 4 years for the vacation-entertainment area and a Disney World entrance of some kind at I-4 and 530, given another 10 years or so for EPCOT to evolve, and given the 10 to 15 million people who will come here by then to stay and play and live—Walt, this will be more than simply a world. This will be a legend's golden kingdom. You are that legend, and here the legend will always live.

Thanks, Walt, for giving me the chance to dream this dream too, and the opportunity to play a small part on this great stage. Life is fleeting, but when it is lived for its challenge and achievement gained by reaching for the stars . . . for giving to the world before you receive from it . . . the rewards are golden indeed, and the legend will never die.

With all respect, forever, and confident that wherever you are, you are driving the devil himself, I remain your most affectionately,

Marty Sklar

Epcot—Planning and Building

The large Epcot model was a fixture in the WDI Model Shop for the duration of the project.

With an aerial shot of Epcot behind him, Marty plays a prank on the cutout image of himself that stood sentinel in his office at Imagineering.

Robert McCall paints *The Prologue and the Promise*, his forward-looking (and later missing) mural for Epcot's Horizons pavilion.

Nothing escaped Marty's review in the lead-up to Epcot's opening. Here, he inspects a specimen in The Land pavilion displaying innovative growing techniques.

In his hard hat, Marty walked the site and photographed the construction's progress.

Disney Legends Orlando Ferrante, John Hench, and Marty take a break, with Spaceship Earth developing in the background.

Epcot Opens!

The British and French Concordes landed simultaneously in celebration of the two countries' respective pavilions opening at Epcot; they then came to a precise halt nose to nose as this image captured by Marty shows.

Marty and Leah enjoyed the Epcot opening ceremonies, with the iconic Spaceship Earth providing the backdrop.

The Wonders of Life pavilion at Epcot closed in 2007, but its opening in 1989 was a happy celebration.

Marty's family proudly attended the gala celebrating Epcot's Grand Opening, including (from the left) Leslie, Helen and Robert Aaron, Leah, Marty, and Howard.

Opening Day was a happy day for everyone who had worked so long to realize Walt's dream.

Kraft CEO William O. Beers, Frank Wells, and Mickey Mouse share a plant grown through hydroponic techniques, at The Land pavilion.

Disney CEO Michael Eisner listens as United Technologies CEO Harry Gray speaks at the opening of The Living Seas pavilion.

Goofy listens attentively while MetLife CEO John Joseph Creedon speaks at the opening of the Wonders of Life pavilion at Epcot.

Euro Disney (now Disneyland Paris)

Marty's famed hat was fully loaded with pins in this photo taken at Disneyland Paris.

The tanks rumbling toward the Champs-Élysées on Bastille Day could be seen and heard—and felt!—from Marty and Leah's hotel room.

Leah often accompanied Marty on trips to the parks, during construction and after their openings. Here they are at Disneyland Paris, with its spectacular castle in the background.

The Château de la Belle au Bois Dormant is the perfect "wienie"—and photo backdrop—at Disneyland Paris, which here is still under construction.

The cold and mud at the site of Disneyland Paris created challenges for the construction workers and onsite Imagineers, but they were always cheered by progress review visits from Marty.

Presenting his second book, *One Little Spark!*, at the UCLA Alumni Association, Marty (second from left) was joined by (left to right) Daniel Jue, Peggie Fariss, Dave Crawford, and Eddie Sotto.

Marty shared Disney stories and signed books for Disney Vacation Club members aboard the *Disney Magic*, here docked at Castaway Cay.

Marty and Leah were the "kids" on a 1970 trip to Hawaii and Japan with Roy O. and Edna Disney, Dick and Ann Irvine, and others. Here Marty is called on to attempt a hula dance at the Polynesian Cultural Center.

Aboard a boat on beautiful Lake Tahoe, Marty photographs his grandchildren making a splash.

While travelling, for work or pleasure, Marty always took plenty of photos. Here he's capturing a view from Main Street in Disneyland Paris.

Marty took this 1971 photo of the company's Gulfstream One before one of his many cross-country flights to Florida.

Wing Chao, longtime Imagineering architect and master planner, met up with Marty in Shanghai for the latest in a series of openings.

Marty had his camera at the ready while viewing the exotic Icelandic landscape. Too bad that roll of film was lost due to the cold!

A little rain couldn't take the smile off of Marty's face while greeting fans at the just-opened Shanghai Disneyland.

Marty made it clear that he approved of the Shanghai park!

project. A design that could work for multiple projects is, to us, a failure for every one of them. We ask a lot of questions, listen to every answer, comb for hints and inspiration on our own—sometimes from a site visit, even if it's just a dirt lot. I like to stand there alone, in silence, feeling and sensing. That's when I can see the project completed . . . and when I know where to begin.

This can happen in one of two ways: either after a struggle of ideas in a multi-person brainstorm with many of the disciplines we utilize to do what we do. Or in a personal flash; when the ideas just rush in on their own.

That happened to me recently. We were working with Universal Studios Hollywood, redoing the interactive fountain we created at CityWalk two decades ago. They wanted to keep it interactive, as that's where its magic lies, but to add something new, which would be refreshing and an exciting new draw, much as the original fountain was when it premiered. (It was the first "fountain" in the world without a body of water and with air-powered water jets shooting right through the pavement floor for kids to run in and through.) When I arrived to meet the client, I pulled into their parking lot, where my attention was grabbed by giant black-and-white murals of classic Universal stars. Among my favorites: Boris Karloff as Frankenstein and Bela Lugosi as Dracula. In a flash, I saw Universal contrasting their great cinematic history with the thrilling films they produce today, now in the richest of colors. I thought of the classic

CityWalk fountain we were about to enhance and thought, "Let's make this same leap forward!" Where the "monochrome" waters had been, we will create liquid color for you to run through, water plumes so intensely saturated that their colors compete with the sun at its peak. The first fountain where you don't wait for dark to see the colors reserved for the darkness of a movie theater.

*In that moment, I knew we had it: the inspiration, the connection, the idea seed from which to create a new wonder to thrill the public all over again. Listening creates all sorts of miracle pills that make everyone **feel great**!*

* * * * * * * * * *

Rick Rothschild has a unique point of view developed by his "inside/outside" experience. After spending thirty-one years *inside* Imagineering—during which time he produced and directed many shows, including The American Adventure in Epcot and Soarin' Over California for Disney California Adventure—Rick moved *outside* in 2009 to create and install projects around the world. That experience led him to work with the creative staffs of many companies and become so well-known that he was elected president of the Themed Entertainment Association. He continues to produce and direct for Disney, as well as major clients in North America, Asia, and the Middle East. Rick says:

The differences I see from my perspective start with an appreciation for institutional memory that naturally develops in a longtime organization like Imagineering.

There is a positive and a negative that comes with this inherent organizational attitude.

On the positive side, an evolved organizational perspective honed from repeated process realizing creative product increases the potential for repeated success. In other words, there becomes a "way" . . . a "Disney way" in how to create and produce a Disney project. On the negative side, this same memory can become an inhibitor, making it difficult to accommodate new, different, and better ways of approaching a creative and/or production challenge.

So, I would say that working inside with outside talent is well worth it. Having access to perspective gained from alternative problem-solving and working environments is quite useful in pursuing new ideas and creative objectives. A specific example of how this consideration affected the casting of a creative team was my challenge to develop a nighttime entertainment district at Walt Disney World, Pleasure Island. It was clear to me as the creative executive that as we were developing a new and unique Disney product, our process would benefit from the infusion of outside perspective blended with the Disney institutional memory. Further, bringing in talent that had no specific affinity for Disney could further enrich the project, helping to push the boundaries of what is "expected" Disney . . . helping to create an unexpected yet still Disney product. The highly successful guest response when we opened Pleasure Island in 1989 expressed what can result from taking advantage of this "inside/outside" collaboration.

Virtually every Disney project team of which I was a part was infused with a variety of outside talent across many disciplines. This blend enriched the final product by bringing different experiences and incredibly useful alternative perspectives, both creatively and technically.

* * * * * * * * * *

Creating shows and attractions for Disney parks is a continuing education for designers and storytellers. We are very fortunate to be able to access the knowledge and expertise of world-renowned authorities—experts through their study and practice of every field and practice you can imagine, disciplines as varied as a university history professor (Epcot) and a world authority in studying the incredible community of insects around the globe (Animal Kingdom).

One of Imagineering's premier senior executives working with the best and brightest experts we could bring together to advise our Imagineering teams was **Barry Braverman**. A teacher by training, Barry had deep curiosity to explore a wide variety of subjects. I asked Barry, now retired from Imagineering, to draw on his experiences in working with our advisory board consultants and write about the challenges and opportunities:

Consultation with content experts from academia and industry was an essential element in the creative development of Epcot's pavilions for several important reasons. First of all, the Imagineers saw their role primarily as entertainers and communicators—skilled at creating captivating and memorable experiences, but definitely not content experts. Secondly, the subjects being addressed in the pavilions were vast in scope, complex, potentially controversial, and critical to the future of the planet. In order for the design teams to begin their work, they needed to connect with experts in disciplines such as communication, energy, transportation, oceanography, agriculture, health, and even imagination. Moreover, each pavilion had a corporate sponsor with very specific messages that they wanted to communicate, which made the involvement of outside advisors critical to ensuring the credibility of the presentation. Finally, the notion of combining the best thinking from universities and laboratories with the magic of Disney storytelling was integral to Walt's original conception of Epcot.

The biggest challenge in implementing the collaboration between outside experts and the design teams was one of distillation. Not surprisingly, when invited to advise Disney Imagineers on what they should be communicating in the pavilions, the outside experts had plenty of input to offer. Their immense storehouses of knowledge, not to mention their academic disagreements, sometimes overwhelmed the designers, who needed clearly delineated, concise "big ideas" that lent themselves to the decidedly nonacademic media of rides, films, and exhibits. In the course of these discussions, which often took the form of periodic advisory board meetings that continued throughout the design process, the Imagineers quickly identified advisors who were not only able to distill complicated content into bite-size chunks, but who were enthusiastic (at times verging on messianic) about the potential for communicating important ideas to the millions of guests who would be visiting Epcot.

One of the most valuable and messianic of these advisors was Dr. Charles (Chuck) Lewis from UCLA, who served as an advisor on the Wonders of Life pavilion. Chuck immediately understood the immense potential of Wonders of Life to communicate powerful messages about health and wellness. He referred to guests' experiences at Epcot as "teachable moments" and preached a doctrine of "an ounce of information in a ton of fun," a sentiment that endeared him to the Imagineers. Chuck passionately embraced the idea that Epcot's critical role was to provide "turn-ons" that would excite guests with the challenges and opportunities of the future and would inspire them to learn more. His contributions to Wonders of Life were numerous and invaluable. He was a devoted fan of Cranium Command, a whimsical attraction that put guests inside the head of a thirteen-year-old boy dealing with the stresses of adolescence. Chuck helped the team focus on the criticality of the fight-or-flight response as a primary cause of stress.

Chuck Lewis also had noticed on his visits to Disneyland that he sometimes encountered young children who were fidgety and cranky and whose parents didn't appear to be fully enjoying The Happiest Place on Earth. Chuck saw that these encounters invariably occurred in queue lines while guests were waiting to board an attraction. His *observations led to a multiyear effort by Imagineers to devise a wide range of queue-line experiences, many specifically designed for young children, to make the wait time pass like "a spoonful of sugar" helping the medicine go down.*

* * * * * * * * * *

I asked one of the most respected people in the theme industry to give me her "general observation" about the creative leadership challenges of shepherding a team of "inside" and "outside" talents. **Pat MacKay** is always in demand to organize an industry event such as the annual TEA Summit Conference. She is a longtime observer of the industry as a journalist; through her company, Ones & Zeros, Pat has spent the last twenty years as a creative content producer. She has organized Women in Technology meetings, focused attention on key issues and industry trends, and fostered leadership training. In 2015, Pat MacKay received the Themed Entertainment Association Distinguished Service Award. She writes:

Leading a team of creatives? Check your ego at the door.

In an ideal world that Dream Team who came up with the genius concept and worked smoothly to opening day on your last project would be available for your next project. But, hey, this is themed entertainment and we specialize in "something going terribly wrong." Just for fun!

Whatever your title—team leader or producer or wizard extraordinaire—protecting your sanity and the sanity of others, so you may live to create genius another day, has to be your top priority. You're the one who has to get everyone on the same page and marching to the same goal all while whistling a happy tune.

Companies in the industry come in all sizes and shapes. The big guys. The boutiques. The in-betweens. And the basic finances of staying in business through ups and downs of financial and real estate cycles require massive flexibility. Companies staff up when they're busy, slim down when they're not. Just about everybody has worked with everybody else at one time or another. We all have history. Not always bright and sunny. But history can also be a good thing because, well, you already know the strengths and weaknesses.

I'm a big fan of management by walking around. I'm always walking by someone's drawing board or desk. How's it going? Anything you need? Did you get that research you needed? When do you think there will be something to look at? What's that you're working on? Oh, wait, there's new input? New scope? How's that going to work into the schedule?

The things you can learn by just walking down the hall to get a cup of coffee can make all the difference between a good idea that's about to go horribly wrong and—yikes!—getting that new technology solution into the hands of a designer before it's too late!

Never underestimate the power of random ideas sparking a creative firestorm in a close working environment.

What will get a creative moving forward—
preferably on time, on budget, and with inspiration?
Frequently it depends on their background. Did they
train in theater? If so, they already know that getting
the show open is a collaborative effort and they will
do whatever it takes. Are they theme park geeks
who are really more interested in doing something
supercool than staying in business and serving
the client? Did they come up through architecture
school or art school? This isn't work for solitary artist
geniuses who love ivory towers. It is a collaborative,
entertainment business endeavor!

And then . . . well, some people I know swear that
there is no way you can actually "manage" creatives
and the creative process. It has a life of its own. But
it's your job to try to corral and channel that process.

And remember the basic rules of the Six Degrees
of Separation Theme Park Game—you'll all be
working together again!

* * * * * * * * * *

One more thought about consulting, from **Roberta Perry**, a former president of TEA, and now vice president of business development for Edwards Technologies: "Every time I am asked to consult on a project or to bring talented teams to the table, I remember my own wise words, [which] I wrote in 2001," Roberta says. "'Congratulations. . . . You have hung up your shingle under the guise of Consultant . . . with a capital C! Now you must bring Knowledge plus Wisdom to the table. Twenty-five years of experience has given you the knowledge; pray you now have the wisdom . . . and hope they have a table!' "

* * * * * * * * * *

To wrap up this chapter, I turn to my longtime colleague **Nancy Seruto**, Portfolio Executive Producer at Imagineering, who beautifully sums up the nature of the collaborative process at Imaingeering:

As I try to pinpoint what makes Imagineering so unique, I would say it is the sheer horsepower of the organization, the overwhelming breadth and depth of expert talent and resources, and the commitment top-down to exceed expectations and break new ground. All opened the way for creating an attraction I never would have dared trying or dreamed possible before.

The volition when you add it all up is enormous, and if you find yourself here in the midst of a large-scale project, then you need to be prepared to discover an entirely new way of working and creating—and of leading. And yes, this means that meetings are large, and communications across so many people take extra effort, but it also means when you hit crunch time, you will be so glad to see each and every one! Finding the best way to tap into so much talent and to rally and align forces around a single mission can feel like leading a small nation at times, but the rush of seeing it all come together is a thrill beyond description.

The second is the organizational pride that oozes

from the corners of places like the model shops, the various plain wrap brown warehouse buildings up and down the block that house truly mind-blowing work, and hallways that have been tread by so many creative people over the decades. It's a sense of collective knowledge over a few generations, the responsibility everyone feels to keep delivering magic to the guests, magic that has permanence and value, and the culture of perfection that perseveres.

It is perhaps that unique tribal appreciation of the power of optimism, and of beauty and quality, that drives the heartbeat of the place.

CHAPTER 7

MOUSE MEETS, MONORAILS, AND ALL THE DISNEY SHIPS AT SEA

The first time I was invited to a "Mouse Meet" in the Pacific Northwest, I did a double—or triple—take, as in, "What's a *Mouse Meet?*" Is there some kind of infestation in the far north? Well, after speaking at two of them, and enjoying the hospitality of Don and Michelle Morin at their Mukilteo, Washington, home, I can say with authority that the "Pacific Northwest Mouse Meet" is as good a Disney fan event as I have ever attended.

The only "mistake" that founder and impresario Don Morin makes each summer is that the barbecue dinner he cooks at his home on Friday before the weekend program makes it very difficult for the speakers to "perform" for the four hundred annual attendees the next day. That fresh-caught salmon, perfectly barbecued by Don, steals the show every time.

In the thirty-five years or so since I accepted that first invitation to speak about Epcot, I have had the pleasure of meeting and speaking to Disney fans across the USA, and as far away as Amsterdam, Paris, Tokyo, and Hong Kong. I've done book signings with actor and comedian Dick Van Dyke (for Mice Chat) and prolific author Ridley Pearson (*Kingdom Keepers, The Return, Peter and the Starcatchers*). The local language may change, but everywhere I speak, "Walt Disney" speaks an *international language.* "Mouse Meet" may be generic, but the Mouse behind the curtain is always Mickey.

Long ago, it ceased to amaze me that so many things we take for granted today in the world of Disney began as an idea or "people-first philosophy" from Walt Disney. The notes I took in meetings with Walt during 1966—for the script I was writing for his film about the concept for the future Walt Disney World and Epcot projects in Florida—said it all: "We have to *meet the needs of the people* who come here," Walt emphasized.

I hold a belief that "meeting the needs of people" is at the heart of all Disney entertainment. That's the way Walt created films, television shows . . . and Disneyland. The words Walt chose for the dedication plaque in Disneyland's Town Square at the opening on July 17, 1955, make this philosophy clear: "To all who come to this happy place: Welcome. Disneyland is your land."

This "philosophy" informed everything I tried to accomplish in my Imagineering career—including my by now numerous talks to Disney fan groups everywhere. That's why I always insisted on providing time at the end of my presentation for a Q and A session—questions from the audience, answers from me and, when they joined me, my fellow Imagineers.

My second book—*One Little Spark! Mickey's Ten Commandments and The Road to Imagineering*—gave me an opportunity to invite some talented Imagineers to join me on stages from Florida to Illinois and multiple venues in California. After all, I had seventy-five Imagineers to choose from—the seventy-five who had each written something about the subjects of chapter headings in the book: Passion, Collaboration, Curiosity, Mentoring, Take a Chance, etc.

Sometimes the Imagineers I asked to participate were there because they were connected to the venue in some way. For example, in two presentations to UCLA alumni groups, I was able to include Bruin alums Daniel Jue, Peggie Fariss, and engineer/R & D executive Dave Crawford in my programs. In Florida, I was joined by three of my favorite associates: Imagineers Daniel Joseph (special effects) and Diego Parras (media relations), and former Imagineer **Steve "Mouse" Silverstein.**

"Mouse" deserves a few paragraphs of his own, because his story is so illustrative of the objectives of many young people. Today "Mouse" is one of the most respected "techies" at Walt Disney World—principal specialist in Design and Engineering. But spin the calendar back to 1981, when I wrote this letter to sixteen-year-old Steve Silverstein (aka "Mouse").

December 22, 1981

Mr. Steve Silverstein

████████████████

Dear Steve:

Ron Miller, President of Walt Disney Productions, sent along to my
attention a copy of a letter from your mother, and an accompanying
article from the Burlington County Times.

I am very impressed by your enthusiasm and dedication, Steve, as
evident by the photographs and accompanying story. You have chosen
some difficult tasks, and that especially is to be encouraged. In
fact, one of my purposes in writing is to encourage you not just to
repeat what Disney has done, but to strike out in your own directions
and stretch your own creative muscles.

This is an important part of the creative process. We have no idea
what the limits of our talents are. In fact, the limits are usually
imposed on us by others; often we impose those limits on ourselves.
So, I hope you will free up your thinking and let your imagination be
your guide.

Please keep in touch as you try new things. Perhaps we can be of
some help or advice. And if you ever get a chance to visit Walt
Disney World or Disneyland, please let me know. Perhaps we can show
you a few things that will stimulate you for your own future
projects. I am also circulating the story from the Burlington County
Times to several members of our staff, so you may be hearing from
them with other ideas.

Have an imaginative and inventive year!

Sincerely,

Martin A. Sklar
Vice President
Creative Development

MAS:tv

cc: Ron Miller

WED ENTERPRISES · Glendale, California, Lake Buena Vista, Florida   HEADQUARTERS · 1401 Flower Street, Glendale, California 91201 · (213) 956-8500
LAKE BUENA VISTA OFFICE · P.O. Box 40, Lake Buena Vista, Florida 32830 · (305) 828-2271

im • ag • i • near'ing,' Imaginative Concepts in Design, Architecture, Engineering and Entertainment – See Disneyland in California and Walt Disney World in Florida
LAKE BUNA VIST VL OFFICE 40, Lake Buena Buena Vista Vista, Fll.

125

Steve Silverstein's "garage project" in his hometown, Willingboro, New Jersey, was about as complex as you could imagine: he was building his own version of an Audio-Animatronics figure. Always wanting to encourage young people with a creative bent, I forwarded my letter to other Imagineers with this note:

December 22, 1981

TO: Wathel Rogers
     Blaine Gibson
     Bill Novey
     Tony Baxter

Please read the attached story, as well as looking at the pictures. I was going to dismiss it as just another kid in love with the parks, but after reading the article, something sparked me to think that this young man might really be worth helping with encouragement, advice, etc. If you agree, why don't you drop him a note yourself offering your own perspective.

Thanks very much.

                                   Marty

MAS:tv
attachment

To MARTY
THANK YOU AGAIN
FOR EVERYTHING!
- MOUSE   Marty Sklar

Wathel Rogers, whom many of us consider "the father of Audio-Animatronics," followed up with this letter to Steve:

WED ENTERPRISES • A Division of Buena Vista Distribution Co., Inc., subsidiary of Walt Disney Productions

January 14, 1982

Mr. Steve Silverstein
████████████████
████████████████

Dear Steve:

I received a copy of your correspondence to our company and the article in the Burlington County Times. It is always a pleasure to hear from someone as interested in our shows as you obviously are.

As you can appreciate, many of our systems have been developed for our particular type of entertainment and there are certain proprietary rights that are not available to the public, and as Mr. Sklar mentioned in his December 22 letter, the creative process required to solve a problem or design is much more important than just copying an existing product.

However, if you have a copy of the August, 1963 issue of National Geographic magazine you might check page 206, (copy enclosed) there is a picture of the Lincoln head showing some of the details. As you can see, the lips are supported by springs that are embedded in the skin. pneumatic actuators that cause the lips to pinch at the corners of the mouth, lift to form a smile, extend to shape an "O" form and "F" etc. We have found all of these functions plus eye blinks etc. are very necessary for the star performer, especially if the figure is observed for any length of time. All movements are designed with simple leverage principals. In the case of the pirate auctioneer, where there are many other figures to divide your attention, it is not necessary to be as complex so we have only used a simple sound synchronized mouth. Also because the beard and moustache would cover the subtle moves. We prefer to use the pose and broad moves of the body to tell the story.

Page one of two

WED ENTERPRISES • Glendale California Lake Buena Vista, Florida   HEADQUARTERS • 1401 Flower Street, Glendale California 91201 • 956-6500
LAKE BUENA VISTA OFFICE • PO Box 40 Lake Buena Vista, Florida 32830 • 828-2271

Im • ag • i • neer'ing,' Imaginative Concepts in Design, Architecture Engineering and Entertainment • See Disneyland in California and Walt Disney World in Florida

(continued on page 128)

The key to designing an AudioAnimatronic figure is to
analyze the role the A.A. actor has in the overall story.
The pose, expression and staging all give life. It is not
always necessary to have all functions to make a figure
tell the story. As you become more involved (as I think
you will) you will find that a very strong simple gesture
will be far more effective than a lot of random unnecessary
complex moves. Also to make a successful life-like figure,
you should study the expressions of faces; a happy face,
a sad face etc. The mechanical and electronic functions
are very important but unless you have a well sculpted
face and figure the end result will be less than satis-
factory. If you do not sculpt or draw and are more
interested in the control systems of the shows, perhaps
you could team up with someone who has that ability. Our
shows are all developed and produced utilizing the talents
of many people.

I hope these ideas may be of some help to you and please
let us know when you visit Epcot in December. I hope you
will enjoy our new shows and find them as stimulating as
our other shows in Walt Disney World.

Sincerely,

Wathel L. Rogers
Director, Show Effects

WLR:egb

Soon after, a star was born—or at least, an intern, age seventeen, joined us at Imagineering. His name was Steve Silverstein, but he has always preferred "Mouse." Recently he summarized his Disney career:

I have over thirty years' experience designing, engineering, and integrating highly complex electronic embedded control systems (microprocessor/ microcontroller-based) and their corresponding hardware/firmware/software for the purposes of animating, programming, and controlling Audio-Animatronics figures and attractions. Walt Disney Imagineering has used these tools, inventions, and devices for programming, animating, and controlling countless Audio-Animatronics figures and attractions in Disney theme parks throughout the world since the late 1980s.

* * * * * * * * * *

I am always blown away listening to his background story when **Alfredo Ayala Jr.** joins me "on the road." Today Alfredo is a principal creative lead in Imagineering's outstanding R & D team—a long road away from the time this fourteen-year-old was caught stealing chemicals by a professor at California State University, Los Angeles!

Imagine this: the son of a master boot-maker who had emigrated from Mexico to Los Angeles, Alfredo recalls the day his mother gave him a single penny to buy a used book at a "penny book sale" conducted by his elementary school library. Why one penny only? "My mother wanted to be sure I chose only the one book that most interested me," Alfredo recalls. The book the fifth grader chose? "I examined every-thing, and chose the one that most intrigued me. It was about atomic energy."

Thus began a fifth grader's interest in science, especially chemistry. Supplies to experiment with chemicals are expensive, especially for a young man from the barrios of East Los Angeles. That's how Alfredo and his friends came to be "borrowing" chemicals from the university . . . and how Alfredo was caught.

The professor wanted to know why "the boys" were stealing chemicals. When he heard about their interest in the world of science, he turned Alfredo over to . . . his parents, and became Alfredo's lifelong mentor and friend. His name: Carlos Gutierrez.

So Alfredo Ayala Jr. majored in chemistry in college. Today he is responsible for leading R & D project teams in "identifying differentiators and adapting and creating new forms of technology and storytelling" to meet the needs of the Imagineers and other divisions of The Walt Disney Company. He holds fourteen patents and has published papers on topics of organic chemistry syntheses and Autonomatronics. In 2011, Alfredo received the Imagen Creative Achievement Award, and he holds membership in the Institute of Electrical and Electronics Engineers, the American Chemical Society, and the American Optical Society.

Alfredo has made important contributions to many of our fans' favorite attractions and restaurants: Soarin', Mission: SPACE, Finding Nemo Submarine Voyage, Radiator Springs Racers in Cars Land, Animator's Palate (on the Disney Cruise Line ships), and many more.

"For me, going to work is going to play," Alfredo says. "I play every day!"

Thank you, Alfredo, for joining my Imagineering travels and panel presentations. And thank you, Professor Gutierrez, for calling young Alfredo's parents—and not the campus police.

* * * * * * * * * *

An article and photo appeared in the July 6, 1992, issue of *Jet* magazine with the headline HAMPTON U. STUDENTS WIN DISNEY ENGINEERING MEET.

"A three-member team of architecture students from Hampton University," the story reads, "recently won Walt Disney Imagineering 'ImagiNations' design competition for minority and female college students."

It listed **Dexter B. Tanksley** as one of the three who "placed first in the competition after presenting their ideas to a panel of specialists from Walt Disney."

That was the start of Dexter Tanksley's career as a designer, architect, and today project design manager at Imagineering. It was Dex who took the initiative to form a team at Hampton to develop a highly themed "indoor ski slope," featuring a character star he called "Dogemite."

"If we had not succeeded," Dex has reflected many times, "I would be designing strip malls in Rochester, New York" (his hometown).

Instead, Dexter progressed from his architectural roots to manage teams in Imagineering's Architectural Studio, responsible for translating ideas of the creative team into dimensional attractions for Disney parks worldwide. He's worked on projects for every Disney park and such signature attractions as Indiana Jones Adventure and Radiator Springs Racers and was the architectural lead for Adventure Isle, one of the six themed lands in Shanghai Disneyland.

I'm especially proud that Dex has taken an active role in the program that gave him the opportunity at Imagineering, serving as chairman of the ImagiNations Advisory Board. I launched this program in 1993 with the objective to diversify Imagineering's staff—seeking new ideas, new talent, and opportunities for women and minority creative talent. Its slogan is "Dream. Design. Diversify." It's a team competition (because that's the way Imagineers work) open to university students from many disciplines—from artists to engineers, designers to computer technicians. In 2017, there were 340 entries from university student teams from the Atlantic to the Pacific, and the Gulf of Mexico to the Canadian border.

Each year, the students are given a specific assignment for the competition. Here's a recent challenge:

Design a travelling experience that will tour small towns across the United States so families who do not have the opportunity to travel to a Disney Park can have a Park experience. This temporary venue will operate in each community for two or three days, should take no more than a day to set up and break down, and embody the kind of family entertainment that Walt envisioned when he first built Disneyland.

Six finalist teams compete for paid internships at Imagineering. In the process of competing, many talented college students have the opportunity to show their talents in their discipline to key Imagineering leaders.

Dex Tanksley has also become a motivational speaker, working with Disney's Dreamers Academy and media personality Steve Harvey for more than a decade, inspiring young talent participating in the program at Walt Disney World. Dex is committed to the program's goals: to plant the seeds of knowledge, inspiration, exposure, and hope in the students attending the Dreamers Academy.

* * * * * * * * * *

One of my favorite programs to participate in, for the past dozen years, is called "Courageous Creativity." It's a "joint venture" between Imagineering, Disneyland, and the California Arts Project, a statewide leadership and professional development center for educators located at California State University, San Bernardino, with a regional network throughout California.

The annual three-day program takes place in June at the Disneyland Resort. It consists of a combination of teaching-related sessions about the arts and tours and presentations by Disney professionals in story, design, music, dance, engineering, etc.

The Courageous Creativity Conferences began when a former Imagineer, the late and talented "creative entrepreneur" Peggy Van Pelt, brought her friend Kris Alexander and me together to discuss ways to inspire and refresh California teachers in the arts. As the executive director of the California Arts Project, Kris's mission is to improve teaching and learning in art, dance, music, theater, visual arts, media, and entertainment. Sound like a match made in heaven? Well, it certainly has been a match made for a magic kingdom! As Kris wrote in a recent program introduction, "We invite you to be courageous and surrender yourself throughout the conference to embrace the dream of future possibilities for the students of California."

It has been my privilege to present the keynote speech opening the conference each year since its beginning in 2006. In 2017, my talk was called "The Challenge of Being the Best That You Can Be—Ten Ways to Motivate and Inspire You to Turn a Challenge into a *New Opportunity.*"

But my favorite event each year is the third day's panel discussion by a group of Imagineers. I have the privilege to be the moderator for the discussion, called "Getting Started on a Career in the Arts." Each of the Imagineers who participates tells his or her personal background story and then shows projects they have helped create for the Disney Parks and Resorts around the world.

I could write a book about the panelists and their amazing accomplishments, but what I want you to read about now are three examples of the twenty-eight different Imagineers who have inspired the educators since the program began.

Shelby Jiggets-Tivoni is the creative and advanced development executive for Disney Parks Live Entertainment. An Imagineer since 2001, Shelby has worked with a number of renowned theatrical artists in producing a variety of imaginative and memorable productions for Disney Parks and Resorts venues, including *Twice Charmed: An Original Twist on the Cinderella Story* (for Disney Cruise Line), *Disney's Aladdin: A Musical Spectacular* (Disney California Adventure), and *Snow White: An Enchanting New Musical* (Disneyland).

I really love hearing Shelby tell the story of her background.

She grew up attending an all-black school in Richmond, Virginia. But through the last vestiges of President Lyndon Johnson's Great Society programs, Shelby was introduced to the worlds of dance, music, and theater. Soon she was on the way to the Big Apple for experiences in theater—everything from ticket taking to her talents in dramaturgy. She contributed to the development of more than thirty American plays and musicals, notably the award-winning *Bring in 'da Noise, Bring in 'da Funk.*

Shelby's journey from segregation in Richmond to the diversity of the Disney Parks theatrical productions (from Anaheim and Aulani in Hawaii to Hong Kong and all the Disney ships at sea) is an inspiration to me, and all the educators. It's a beautiful fit with the event's title, Courageous Creativity.

We really missed **Scot Drake** on our panel for three years when he relocated to Shanghai to lead the design of Tomorrowland there. Scot graduated from the highly respected ArtCenter College of Design in Pasadena, California, where he was exposed to the work of such luminaries of advanced design as Syd Mead, the influential designer whose work is featured in the films *Blade Runner, TRON,* and *Alien.* Syd Mead once said, referencing his designs, "I've called science fiction 'reality ahead of schedule.'"

I really enjoyed Scot's approach to his team's challenge in Shanghai Disneyland's Tomorrowland. Before the park's opening, Scot told me, "I am most excited to share the hope and optimism Disney has for the future with an audience that is charging into the future every day here in Shanghai. I truly believe that Disney has always had a responsibility to showcase how creativity will shape us into a better tomorrow.

135

Shanghai's Tomorrowland will showcase a harmony of mankind's creativity and curiosity, mixed with beauty, comfort, and the design philosophies we are constantly learning from nature."

Now that Scot is back at Imagineering in Glendale (leading the design of new Disney–Marvel franchise attractions), we welcomed him back to our Courageous Creativity panel to tell the story of his experiences in China—including the adoption of a Chinese-born son. He and his wife and daughter returned from Shanghai in a slightly larger family unit.

Scot's tales really hit home with the educators attending Courageous Creativity: he readily admits that he was the kid in the back of the room doodling and drawing regardless of the lesson of the day. Scot designed the Mark VII Disneyland Monorail, murals that have brought the exterior of whole buildings to life, and the TRON Lightcycles. When he talks about the need and the challenge of keeping even "the nerds" of a typical classroom interested without killing that spark of creativity, it really resonates with teachers.

And it has thrilled me beyond words to watch a young talent like Scot Drake grow over those dozen years in his ability not only to conceive and draw his dream ideas, but to articulate and present them in ways that motivate and inspire others.

And by the way, Scot also teaches Digital Painting for Entertainment and Visual Communication at his alma mater, ArtCenter in Pasadena.

* * * * * * * * * *

Sometimes it's hard to define the "chemistry" that draws you to one talented person's path to success in his or her field over others. But as soon as I heard **Daniel Joseph**'s story, I knew we had to include him on our Courageous Creativity panel.

Now principal special effects designer for Imagineering, leading a department based at Walt Disney World, Daniel was once shunned by his young classmates, who thought he was a slow learner in core studies. But Daniel loved to play with his gadgets and electrical experiments. One day he brought his latest "toy" to school—and amazed his critics with his knowledge and know-how. They quickly recognized his skills as an inventor whose learning process and interests just happened to be very different from theirs.

Daniel is another winner of the ImagiNations design competition. He majored in industrial design at the University of the Arts in Philadelphia. Today he is listed as an inventor on twenty-five patents—one of them named "one of the best inventions of 2011" by *PC Magazine*.

It's another great story for the teachers to hear—especially when that "slow student" talks about one of his recent assignments: creating special effects for Disney's new Star Wars–themed lands. He's been working at "light speed" to create iconic visuals.

* * * * * * * * * *

There's a special place in this part of the Courageous Creativity story for **Kevin Rafferty**. He's always been the "cleanup act"—the last to speak—on these panels because: (a) he's got so much to say, (b) nobody says it with so much enthusiasm, and (c) he's very funny!

Kevin's another Imagineer whose background jumps out at you and serves as a great lesson. A graduate of California

State University, Fullerton, who wanted to become a Disney animator, Kevin took a giant step in that direction with his first job at Disneyland: washing dishes at the Plaza Inn restaurant. But as his father told him, "The only place you'll find success before work is in the dictionary."

Today as an executive creative director for Imagineering, Kevin is one of the most prolific "idea people" at Imagineering—writer, songwriter, producer, director for dozens of Disney park shows. Secretly, I think his favorite is a Cars Land gem—Radiator Springs Racers—in Disney California Adventure, but I love some of his offbeat shows: Sonny Eclipse (the Biggest Little Star in the Galaxy) for Tomorrowland at the Magic Kingdom; the Pan Galactic Pizza Port in Tomorrowland in Tokyo Disneyland; and It's Tough to Be a Bug! at Disney's Animal Kingdom.

What a message for all of us: "Everything begins somewhere," even if it's washing dishes!

* * * * * * * * * *

As I write this, I'm about to walk out the door of my home office and make the ten-minute drive from the Hollywood Hills to the UCLA campus in Westwood. It seems serendipitous that when Cia Ford, senior director of Professional School and Affinity programs at UCLA, e-mailed me in June to inquire if I would speak at a new series at the James West Alumni Center, she wrote that I would be "the second act" in a new series featuring UCLA alumni. The program is called "2nd Act"—created to feature Bruin grads whose careers have had a second flowering—mine being as an author and speaker whose degree in political science did not lead to politics or law.

Returning to the UCLA campus—so vastly different today than in the 1950s when I was an undergraduate—is at once a culture shock and a thrill. A culture shock because in the early fifties UCLA was a commuter campus full of stay-at-homes and renters of nearby apartments. Until 1959, there was just one women's dorm and no (as in *zero*) men's dorms. A thrill because today UCLA receives more applications for admission than any other school in the country—about a hundred thousand for 5,900 freshman spots in 2017. And there are seventeen high-rise towers and five low-rise dorms housing eleven thousand students on "the hill" across from the main campus.

The compliment Cia Ford and the UCLA Alumni Association are paying me through this invitation made me think about other venues and hosts where I have had the opportunity to "sing my song" about my books to audiences from sea to shining sea. In addition to Don Morin and the Pacific Northwest Mouse Meet, here are a few of my favorites:

Chicago's Museum of Science and Industry (MSI): This historic museum is housed in one of the world's great museum structures. It was built as the Palace of Fine Arts for the 1893 World's Columbian Exposition. Today it houses an incredible array of historic and scientific experiences that range from a walk-through German U-boat (submarine) from World War II to a full-size replica coal mine, and temporary exhibits such as Robot Revolution.

Years ago, museum president and CEO David Mosena made a brilliant hire—my friend and former Imagineer Kurt Haunfelner. I had known Kurt since he was at Loara High

School in Anaheim and college at California State University, Fullerton, and watched him grow into one of the "new breed" of museum producers, creating experiences to stretch the minds of younger visitors—incorporating theme park techniques and unusual ways to convey information. In fact, several of Kurt's museum productions have earned the Thea Award for Outstanding Museum Exhibits from TEA—including Science Storms.

I spoke at MSI about my first two books to an astonishing (to me, at least!) sold-out audience of seven hundred people. What enthusiasm—especially when Alfredo Ayala and Dex Tanksley joined me for my second visit. After we spoke, it seemed as though everyone in Chicago wanted to talk to us, have us sign the books they purchased, and take a selfie with us. In fact, we signed and made small talk for *five hours*! (I think if Dex had not been hungry, we would still be there!)

Perhaps more than at any other venue, those two afternoons at the Museum of Science and Industry in Chicago made me realize how important we Imagineers are as "ambassadors" of the Disney spirit and culture. How else to characterize the desire of so many Disney fans to hear us, meet us, shake our hands, and remember the experience with a selfie?

It was in Chicago in 2014 that I met the Kelley family from the Cleveland, Ohio, area for the first time. Actually, I met fifteen-year-old Jacob Kelley first; he followed me around the museum as I enjoyed a guided tour by Kurt Haunfelner. It seemed as though every time we stopped, Jacob was there with another perceptive question. Then after I spoke, at the book signing, his parents explained that they had driven all the way from Cleveland *that day* so that Jacob could hear my talk—and, of course, ask me innumerable questions. And they were driving back *that evening*—all 336 miles!

Jacob Kelley and I have become "pen pals" over the years since—if that's what we call e-mail correspondents these days. Jacob was fixated from the beginning on his goal—to become an Imagineer or a Disney animator. Early in 2017, I connected Jacob with Jason Grant, a writer and designer at Imagineering in Florida working on future projects for Epcot, and Mk Haley, whose counsel you will find in the "Best Advice" chapter. They helped Jacob, who at the time was about to graduate from high school, with his plan to attend a community college in the Orlando area, and "get his feet wet" (no Florida pun intended!) by working part-time as a cast member at Walt Disney World.

Believe me, it's a thrill to play a role in the growth of talented young people. I have told them all a couple of simple lessons: when you are young, learn as much as you can about as many things as you can; and experience as many positive things as you can handle—you never know which will be the *one* you want to live in creatively as you "go out into the world." You'll never know what you missed if you don't try!

Fort Worth Museum of Science and History: I'm so proud of my former Imagineering staff members who have accomplished wonderful things after leaving Disney with a great foundation for future endeavors. One of my favorites is Van Romans, now president of the Fort Worth Museum of Science and History.

When we determined that a key component of a visit to the countries represented in Epcot's World Showcase would be "galleries" that depicted various aspects of a nation's culture—art, history, indigenous people, etc.—Van got the job. He became the face and voice of Epcot and the Imagineers to museums, government ministries of antiquities, and private collectors. One example: through Van's diplomacy, our China pavilion gallery was the first location in the United States to display tomb soldiers and horses dating from 210 BCE.

We "loaned" Van to help the Texas Cowboy Hall of Fame in Fort Worth, and it wasn't long after that that the prime supporters of that city's museums came calling with a great offer to become president of their Science and History Museum. Van has since become the shepherd of several major building projects that have transformed the museum—engaging the talented Mexican architect Ricardo Legorreta to create a new main building complex and working with Bob Weis's Design Island firm to create new exhibits. (Since that collaboration, Bob Weis returned to Imagineering to head the Shanghai Disneyland project and is now president of Walt Disney Imagineering.)

It was fun for me to speak at Van's museum about *One Little Spark!* in 2016. I wanted Fort Worth to know how much I respected Van Romans, so I insisted that we engage in a dialogue onstage before the sold-out audience of four hundred. Our banter was the kind of talk friends engage in—an easy conversation that only strayed when it came to our college rivalry: Van's a USC Trojan, and yours truly a UCLA Bruin; we're participants in one of the biggest of big-city rivalries. Civil war was avoided—but Van made me pay afterwards: I signed books for four hours, long into the Fort Worth night.

I applaud Van not only for his leadership turning a good museum asset into a great community service, but especially for engaging and inspiring youngsters. The museum had a long history of educational services, but Van has broadened its offerings and made education exciting and relevant. On the day I visited the program and classes, there was a buzz in all the activities in the building—and it wasn't from bees. Those kids were *engaged*! I was thrilled to watch and listen to the excitement of young people *learning*. That's a "sound" you can hear for miles!

Two more of my favorite book stops have very different personalities—each engaging their communities in far different ways. They represent my coast-to-coast speaking odyssey.

Scott Rodas has left the **Ocean County Library** in Toms River, New Jersey, but as a big Disney fan, he had championed two separate visits to this excellent county facility on the Jersey shore. It was especially fun to have my cousin Suzanne Torrisi and her husband, Vic, and family in the audience; my good friends Chuck and Janet Schmidt were also in attendance. Chuck, the longtime editor of the *Staten Island Advance*, now writes his own blog, whose name reveals all you need to know about Chuck Schmidt. It's called *Goofy About Disney*.

I'll always feel a debt of gratitude to Scott Rodas and the Ocean County Library for two reasons: first, it was my very first stop on my book tour for my first book, *Dream It! Do It!* And second, for how engaged the young members of the audience were. Several came prepared with a special treat for this travelling Imagineer.

From: Reese Willis
9 years old

Thanks to all you young artists for picking up a pencil, a crayon, or a brush and getting started. Your parents and teachers will be thrilled—and you will love all the doors it will open for the future. And if it's dance or music or writing you try—go for it. Fill that blank page or dance floor with *you* . . . and to repeat what Daniel Jue wrote in *One Little Spark!*, "Love what you do—and someday you may do what you love."

Skirball Cultural Center: I first met Rabbi Uri Herscher and his wife, Dr. Myna Herscher, when the Skirball Cultural Center was "just an idea," and Uri and his team needed advice for a proposed "theme exhibit" about immigration to the United States. Disney president Frank Wells asked me to put together a group of Imagineers—with the proviso that we could not spend any money! So my "volunteers"—Larry Gertz, Barry Braverman, Doris Hardoon Woodward, Rick Rothschild, and Leah—met over many lunches in Edie's Conference Room at Imagineering to "brainstorm" ideas for what became the Skirball Cultural Center. (To this day, Dr. Herscher reminds me that every meeting ended with the same reward—chocolate chip cookies from our Big D cafeteria!)

Uri D. Herscher is a scholar, administrator, and rabbi whose commitment to Jewish values has infused the Skirball Cultural Center's dynamics since its inception in 1996. Under his founding vision and leadership, attendance has grown to more than six hundred thousand annually, including eighty thousand schoolchildren (who often visit on field trips). The Skirball's mission is to engage the diverse communities of Southern California—frequently focusing on the contributions of immigrants from many lands and cultures to the character and fabric of our nation.

Uri Herscher's background is informative. He was born in Tel Aviv, Israel, in 1941 to German Jewish refugee parents who fled Hitler's rise to power; his grandparents and many relatives were murdered in Nazi death camps. Dr. Herscher's family immigrated to the United States in the 1950s; he attended the University of California, Berkeley, as an undergraduate, and was later ordained as a rabbi. After receiving his doctorate in American Jewish history in 1970, he became executive vice president and dean of faculty at the four-campus Hebrew Union College–Jewish Institute of Religion in Los Angeles.

With the financial support of the philanthropist couple Jack Skirball and Audrey Skirball-Kenis, Dr. Herscher enlisted one of the world's great architects, Israeli/Canadian/American Moshe Safdie, to design the Skirball Cultural Center. Safdie had achieved fame with his design of Habitat 67 at the Expo 67 world's fair in Montreal, Canada. He has been the one and only architect for the Skirball—and his other works include Yad Vashem, the World Holocaust Remembrance Center in Jerusalem; Kauffman Center for the Performing Arts in Kansas City, Missouri; and Musée de la Civilisation, Quebec City, Canada.

With the expert assistance of Amina Sanchez, then associate director of programs for the Skirball, I kept in mind the diversity Dr. Herscher has championed when I asked Alfredo Ayala, Dex Tanksley, Shelby Jiggets-Tivoni, and Daniel Joseph to join me on the panel discussing their backgrounds. (Of course, I could take this group *anywhere* . . . but it had special meaning in "the house that Uri and Myna built.")

* * * * * * * * * *

As you can imagine, there's a special place on my travel list—and in my heart—for **The Walt Disney Family Museum**, located in the Presidio of San Francisco, part of the Golden Gate National Recreation Area.

The museum was created as a tribute from Diane Disney Miller and her family to Diane's father, Walt Disney. As much as the man and the company he founded with brother Roy O. Disney in 1923 can never be separated, Diane wanted a place that would focus on the *man* who built one of the great entertainment empires in the whole world. So she and her husband, Ron Miller, and the Miller family, chose to locate their tribute away from the home of the movie and TV industry in Burbank, Glendale, and Hollywood. The transformation of the prestigious Presidio area from a military enclave to civilian use made it possible to build The Walt Disney Family Museum there.

Opened in 2009, the museum is a true "brush with Disney"—a dynamic look at the enormous variety of Walt Disney's creations, awards, and lasting impact around the world. A visitor can reminisce over past treasures—the creation of animated films under Walt's baton from *Steamboat Willie* to *The Jungle Book*—to the story of Disneyland and future plans Walt had started, notably his vision for the community he called EPCOT—Experimental Prototype Community of Tomorrow. Plan on spending *hours* when you go; it's entertaining, educational, and (Walt would love this) *fun!*

The museum also presents wonderful in-depth special shows of great Disney artists: Mary Blair, Tyrus Wong, Marc Davis, Eyvind Earle, Andreas Deja, and an almost weekly series of talks about Disney, with an emphasis on "Walt's tune." That's where I enter the picture.

I have had the honor of making a major presentation at The Walt Disney Family Museum on seven or eight occasions, both as a lone presenter (most recently in a program titled "The Challenge of Being the Best You Can Be," featuring the wisdom of Walt and Coach John Wooden, whose UCLA basketball teams won ten NCAA championships in a twelve-year span) and as a group presenter (with Bob Gurr and former Imagineer Frank Stanek about the New York World's Fair; and with Frank, Tony Baxter, and Tom Morris about the opening of the first three international Disney Parks and Resorts locations in Tokyo, Paris, and Hong Kong. Each of my fellow presenters played major roles in their respective projects).

Travelling to San Francisco is never a chore, of course—the city by the bay is one of the world's great cosmopolitan areas, renowned for wonderful scenery, restaurants, sports teams, and museums. Put The Walt Disney Family Museum high on that list. The place and the *man* deserve it.

In the fall of 2016, I was surprised one day when Ron Miller, once my boss when he was president of The Walt Disney Company, called to tell me the museum wanted to present me with its second Diane Disney Miller Lifetime Achievement Award—which I accepted at a wonderful gala event on November 1, 2016, at the Grand Californian Hotel, with Neil Patrick Harris as the master of ceremonies. To "follow" Richard Sherman—the first recipient of this award—put me in some very special company.

* * * * * * * * * *

I had so much fun, and so many experiences, "Travelling with Figment" around the globe. I've told my stories to Disney Vacation Club members aboard the Disney *Magic* with the club's *Disney Files* magazine editor Ryan March acting as moderator, interviewer, and master of ceremonies. I've shared them with the high school students in the Ryman Arts program that Leah and I founded almost thirty years ago with Sharon Disney Lund, Buzz and Anne Price, and Lucille

Ryman Carroll; we've had more than thirty thousand talented young artists in our program, all at no cost to them. I've recounted them to everyone from Troy Carlson and fans of his Stage Nine Entertainment Store in Old Sacramento . . . to attendees of the annual convention of IAAPA (International Association of Amusement Parks and Attractions), where Bob Rogers, chairman of BRC Imagination Arts, and I have presented a panel for almost fifteen years. We call it Things That Never Grow Old.

CHAPTER 8

EVERYTHING I NEED TO KNOW I LEARNED FROM MICKEY'S TEN COMMANDMENTS

Editor's Note: As those of you who've read Marty's other two books know, he first put Mickey's Ten Commandments down on paper in 1983. At the time he was preparing for two major presentations, to the Association of Science-Technology Centers and to the Boston Art Directors' Club. Mickey's Ten Commandments were an attempt to boil down to a few principles the key lessons he had learned from Walt Disney in his first ten years with the company, lessons that had continued to influence him and inform his work throughout the nearly three decades he had already spent at Disneyland and Imagineering by that point. Little did he know then that the commandments would become the guidepost not only for the Imagineers, but throughout the themed entertainment industry.

Before Marty passed away, he asked for contributions for this book. Some of the contributions were submitted before

Marty's death. Others came in later when we let every-one know we were working to complete this book. Here is Marty's original request.

A Request from Marty

I'm in the last stages of a new book as a follow-on to *"Dream It! Do It!"* and *"One Little Spark!"* It will be pub-lished late next year by Disney Editions.

This new book is basically about travelling and speak-ing to all kinds of audiences in the USA, and around the world. When I first started speaking to conventions, con-ferences, corporations and Disney fan groups in the early 1980's, I developed *"Mickey's Ten Commandments"* as a theme, structure and identity. As you know, it became what *Funworld* called "a classic—perhaps the best guide to the creation of themed entertainment."

Whether that's true or not, as the last chapter in my new book, I'm planning a few pages of comments on *the impact of "Mickey's Ten Commandments"* from leaders of the TEA industry. I would love to include your thoughts—anything from a paragraph to a few paragraphs . . . how-ever you would characterize the impact, value and use of "Mickey's Ten Commandments."

Of course, if they have had no impact or use by you and your associates, I would appreciate it if you would keep your mouth shut!

I'm looking to put this last chapter together in early August. So if you are willing/interested in commenting, please get your thoughts to me by August 1.

Thanks much for considering my request!

Marty

1. **KNOW YOUR AUDIENCE**
   Identify the prime audience for your attraction or show before you begin design.
2. **WEAR YOUR GUESTS' SHOES**
   Insist that your team members experience your creation just the way guests do it.
3. **ORGANIZE THE FLOW OF PEOPLE AND IDEAS**
   Make sure there is a logic and sequence in your stories and in the way guests experience them.
4. **CREATE A WIENIE (VISUAL MAGNET)**
   Create visual "targets" that lead visitors clearly and logically through the experience you've built.
5. **COMMUNICATE WITH VISUAL LITERACY**
   Make good use of color, shape, form, texture—all the nonverbal ways of communication.
6. **AVOID OVERLOAD—CREATE TURN-ONS**
   Resist the temptation to overload your audience with too much information and too many objects.
7. **TELL ONE STORY AT A TIME**
   Stick to the story line; good stories are clear, logical, and consistent.
8. **AVOID CONTRADICTIONS—MAINTAIN IDENTITY**
   Details in design or content that contradict one another confuse an audience about your story and its time period.
9. **FOR EVERY OUNCE OF TREATMENT, PROVIDE A TON OF TREAT**
   In our business, Walt Disney said, you can educate people—but don't tell them you're doing it! Make it fun!
10. **KEEP IT UP (MAINTAIN IT)!**
    In a Disney park or resort, everything must work. Poor maintenance is poor show!

If a thirty-year career in business—and more narrowly that bubble called Hollywood (particularly in its intersection with the world of technology)—has taught me anything, it is that the first commandment remains the driving force behind every idea, every pitch, every production, and ultimately every execution of any dream. Having the right answer is never as important as making sure it is the right answer for your audience. Businesses have come and gone, relationships have shattered, projects have failed, new product launches have fizzled, political movements have faltered, and massive elections have been lost when arrogance gets in the way of reality. Knowing, catering to, and, most of all, respecting your audience is the key to connecting with them. You can never reach whatever goals you've set if you can't make that fundamental connection. Knowing your audience remains, for me, the most important of Mickey's Ten Commandments and the driving force in everything I've done since my Imagineering days.

*—**Dan Adler,** Former Vice President, Creative Development, Walt Disney Imagineering*

In the summer of 1993, I became part of an organization that would forever change my life. That organization was Walt Disney Imagineering and at the time, the creative visionary leading this incredible organization of Imagineers was Marty Sklar. My indoctrination included a deep dive into the Disney history, values and Mickey's Ten Commandments.

My initial take on Mickey's Ten Commandments, was that this is the secret sauce to the success of The Walt Disney Company and a recipe to creating our theme parks around the world. It was not until Marty Sklar illuminated the existence of Mickey's Ten Commandments that it became as clear as the blue sky and more importantly why they exist.

Marty Sklar was embarking on one of his book-signing tours for One Little Spark!, and had invited two coauthor Imagineers (Dexter Tanksley and myself) to join him on several of his book-signing events. This was an incredible and humbling experience for me. The opportunity of a lifetime to spend one-on-one time with my idol and friend Marty Sklar. At one event, guests waited for six hours to meet Marty and us and have us sign their books. I glanced over at Marty to suggest a break after three hours of greeting guests and signing their books. Marty turned to me, smiled, and leaned over, then whispered, "Alfredo, we are delivering the promise, 'Walk in their shoes.'" We did the six hours without taking a break. At dinner that night we talked about Mickey's Ten Commandments, and it was then that I understood their true meaning. Marty was not just building a framework for creating successful theme parks, he was solidifying the core motivation to always evolve and stay relevant.

Mickey's Ten Commandments are guiding principles that are universally applied to everything we do. They extend to every design and the delivery *of immersive storytelling and experiences to our diverse guests around the globe.*

Thank you, Marty; I am forever in your debt.

*—**Alfredo Ayala Jr.**, Executive, Research and Development, Walt Disney Imagineering*

Having worked with Marty for almost my entire career, I got to know him as a master of words and as a polished verbal thinker. Marty was keenly aware of the need for cohesive team building and occasionally brought in psychologists and organizational planners to help keep the diverse culture of Imagineering working in harmony. It was during one of these sessions that I became aware that my personal creative abilities had a distinct visual orientation. I would need to develop additional communication techniques to successfully pair up with those whose forte was in the power of words to tell stories.

*With that background, my perception of "Mickey's Ten Commandments" stems from this visually oriented perspective. I'll begin with the five commandments intuitive to most creators of visually successful experiences. They are key to my own professional success. First: **"Know your audience"** . . . A successful experience designer needs to be a member of the potential audience. If they are, it can eliminate the second-guessing about what "those people" might like. **"Wear your guests' shoes"** . . . This is an adjunct to the first. As part of your audience, it goes without saying that you are* keenly aware of audience frustrations as well as their joys. **"Create a wienie (visual magnet)"** . . . A visual thinker sees physical manifestations the way a verbal thinker perceives plot and high concept. **"Avoid overload—create turn-ons"** . . . A visual thinker employs the tools of light, color, sound, music, and thrill to communicate a well-orchestrated experience. In an environmental attraction, words often take a back seat to kinetics, and therefore theatrical tools often communicate better to an audience in motion. Music can be especially effective—can you envision Harry Potter without hearing the John Williams theme? Or can you think of "it's a small world" without hearing the Sherman brothers' music? **"Avoid contradictions—maintain identity"** . . . Professional illustrators, painters, landscape designers, etc. are trained in the art of visual clarity.

The next three commandments are not intuitive to visual thinking and require conscious restraint to avoid the pitfalls of not giving them their due. **"Organize the flow of people and ideas"** . . . Orchestrating people and ideas is critical. The initial phases of a project require open thinking and big ideas. It is a time to stray from formulas and engage with those who revel in upsetting the apple cart. Projects move through stages where a variety of skilled experts are needed, and finally, when a great idea gets locked, detail-oriented thinkers should be on board to push projects over the top. Often details are piled on at the beginning, and they can easily "gild and mask" a less than perfect project. **"Tell one story at a** time" and "Communicate with visual literacy" . . . These two commandments should be fused in visual storytelling. Starting with a vision usually defines the overarching concept. As the concept takes physical dimension, story points are dropped in sequentially to build an adventure told in motion through physical space. Again, color, light and dark, music and sound add variety to spaces, thus defining events occurring in kinetic environments. It's very easy to fall in love with too many good ideas and confuse the audience. 3-D models are an antidote, allowing designers to catch and eliminate "story overload" before it's costly.

"Ounce of treatment—ton of treat" . . . This stand-alone commandment is best illustrated with one of the original attractions at Disneyland Park, Peter Pan's Flight. It only has one critical line of dialogue: Peter's "Come on, everybody, here we go!" From that point, guests create their own impressions of flying off to Neverland. To paraphrase writer Ray Bradbury to Walt Disney, "I will be eternally grateful that you allowed me to fly out of a bedroom window over moonlit London in a pirate galleon on its way to the stars!"

Finally, "Keep it up (maintain it)" . . . This last commandment is so important, but is usually not in the hands of those responsible for creation. Unlike film, where a video disc freezes the final product for all time, an attraction is subject to all kinds of issues as time goes by. Maintenance should be given the same attention as it is on a Broadway play, which is not always the case. In addition, it is crucial to refresh aging attractions to keep them relevant to a *changing demographic. For show business success, this tenth commandment becomes the key factor to establishing the integrity between the purveyor and their audience.*

*—**Tony Baxter,** Disney Legend*

Throughout the development of the Tokyo Disneyland Expansion, the largest expansion ever in the history of that park, we have referenced the commandments frequently. When there is a tough decision to be made, I'll take a look at that list of commandments to find a bit of wisdom. Here are a few thoughts on the lasting impact of the Ten Commandments.

***Know your audience:** Marty succinctly defined our audience as "the family that does things together," and this description is apt at all of our parks around in the world. Know your audience also means know how your audience is evolving. Japan has an aging population and it is becoming even more important that our attractions are available to all members of the family: Mom, Dad, and the kids, but also Grandma and Grandpa. When we set out to create a new "E-ticket" attraction experience for Tokyo Disneyland, this presented a unique challenge. Most of our newer E-ticket attractions include both a height requirement and health restrictions. We were determined to create a dynamic new attraction that had complex, programmable movement like our most sophisticated thrill rides, but could still be enjoyed by the very young and the young at heart. Enchanted Tale of Beauty and the Beast was the answer to this* challenge; a true E-ticket attraction that is fun for the whole family.

Wear your guests' shoes: When my kids were little, we went to Disneyland almost every weekend. When my daughter, Moira, was about four years old, one of the must-do attractions was Walt Disney's Enchanted Tiki Room. However, we always had to sit on an end seat near the door, because as soon as the "drumming guys" began their performance, we had to make a hasty retreat. The drumming guys, after all, angered the gods, which brought about the darkness and the thunderstorm. We repeated this ritual a few dozen times before Moira, at age five, decided she was ready to face the storm. Face it she did, and lived to tell the tale. There is something reassuring about facing your fears and surviving. From roller coasters to Haunted Mansions, Disney parks afford children many opportunities to experience ritual rites of passage. Commandment number two, Wear your guests' shoes, is vital for any theme park professional. I've worn the shoes of many different kinds of guests, but the memory of my time wearing the shoes of a parent are the most valuable. Ten years after Moira first survived the wrath of the tiki gods, I'm still thinking back to those days. As we are creating Enchanted Tale of Beauty and the Beast for Tokyo Disneyland—an attraction set in a dark, spooky castle, where we find a monstrous beast— we need to remember not to make the attraction so scary that it will terrify the small children we are hoping to entertain. On the other hand, just a bit *of a fright is not only welcome, it's essential.*

Create a wienie (visual magnet): *The Beauty and the Beast Castle at Tokyo Disneyland presented a unique challenge. For the first time in Disney park history, we were faced with the task of creating a second full-scale European castle in a park that already had a castle as the centerpiece. We had to be very careful that this new "wienie" did not overpower the park centerpiece, while still serving as an effective visual magnet—both drawing guests toward it and telling them something about the adventure that awaited them inside. Since Cinderella Castle is bright and charming, we decided that our new Beauty and the Beast Castle would be the dark and enchanted version—complete with mist rising up from the moat and a gaggle of goofy gargoyles staring down at the guests as they approach. Cinderella Castle is painted in warm browns, while the Beauty and the Beast Castle is painted in cooler colors. We were also careful not to upstage the symbol of the park; Cinderella Castle stands fifty-one meters tall, while the Beauty and the Beast Castle is about two-thirds its size at thirty-three meters tall.*

—**Jim Clark,** Creative Development Producer, Walt Disney Imagineering

I recall the first time Marty shared Mickey's Ten Commandments (MTC) with me. It was when I was leading design process for DisneyQuest at Walt Disney World in the mid-1990s. At the time we were in final decision mode on DQ and struggling

for cohesiveness in what was a first of its kind Imagineering project. Marty thought MTC would help, and he was (of course) right. I was immediately taken by the balance between clarity of guidance and openness to interpretation in MTC—so characteristic of interactions with Marty. Using MTC as a lens at a subsequent all-hands DQ design review, it was pivotal in helping us see with new eyes: the guest experience we were seeking for our target tween/teen guests and their families; the clear and compelling story environment we wanted to create; and the comfortable and easy ways to navigate the flow we wanted, balancing discovery with certainty. After that meeting it was off to the races!

More than a decade later I shared another impactful MTC experience with Marty. I was a newly minted adjunct professor, teaching a course in New Product Development to MBA students at the UC Davis Graduate School of Management. I had asked Marty to serve as a guest speaker for the class focused on concept development. Marty was (of course, again) enthralling—my students could not get enough of his tales of Walt, opening day at Disneyland, building Epcot, and everything that happened since. As his talk progressed the students were all but smitten—Marty had in a few short minutes achieved rock-star status. As he began to wrap up his talk, he shared the Ten Commandments, framing them as the principles Imagineering had learned were vital to understanding how to create a captivating guest experience. My students were *absolutely blown away to see something as complex as the design of a theme park framed in such succinct and direct terms. It was far and away the most compelling talk of the course, one in which the students came away with not just an understanding of how Imagineering delivers its magic, but also how experience, thoughtfulness, and deeply organized insights could deliver invaluable guidelines and wisdom for their future endeavors.*

*—**Joe DiNunzio**, Executive Director of the UC Davis Institute for Innovation and Entrepreneurship*

What I've always liked about Mickey's Ten Commandments is how they can be applied to more than theme park design.

I've had two careers in my life. The first was in theme parks, working on some really incredible projects at Walt Disney Imagineering, Universal, and Warner Bros.

My second career was journalism, starting in 1997 (both in television news and in print/online). I found that the principles espoused in the commandments could be applied there as well.

I've picked three to expand on this thought.

***Wear your guests' shoes:** For theme parks, that means getting out of the ivory tower of design and walking around as the guests (customers) do at the theme parks. Understand what they are experiencing and where it works well, and apply that understanding to the next project.*

When covering stories for news, it means talking

to people that are directly affected by a news story and relating that information and reaction in the story—in effect, taking the readers (or viewers) to the event (in others' shoes) so they can better understand what happened and how it impacts them and society.

Create a wienie (visual magnet): In theme parks this should be straightforward. Give the guests a reason to further explore the parks, or continue into an attraction, shop, restaurant, or other adventure. In the news, that means (hopefully) a video or photo that helps paint a picture of a story. But it also means, when writing the story, creating a lede (wienie) that gets readers or viewers to follow the story to its end.

Keep it up (maintain it): It should go without saying that if a park or attraction is not maintained, guests will notice it—creating a negative image in their minds. They will tell others, and before long, people will stop coming and the turnstiles will stop clicking.

For journalists, that means keeping the stories fresh and up to date. With the immediacy of social media and its effects on the news cycle, this has become an enormous challenge to the news business.

—**Mark Eades,** Former Imagineer and Journalist

When I first began to attend presentations as a Disney representative in 1974, several of these were at various technical organizations in Detroit. I was appalled at how the professional lecturers would

quickly put their audiences to sleep. Eventually,
I found that good public speaking needs good
design. When Marty Sklar showed me Mickey's
Ten Commandments, I had a template to follow.
The recent decades have been easy, for both me
and the audience. We both get immediately into a
sharing back-and-forth rhythm so naturally. Marty's
methods absolutely work. I can offer two additional
commandments: Always Look Your Guests in the
Eye, and Be on the Lookout for a Sleeping Back Row.
Afterward, you'll both leave happy.

　　　　　　　　　　　　　　　—Bob Gurr, Disney Legend

I have had Mickey's Ten Commandments framed
and on the wall in my office for more than twenty
years. We preach these commandments almost daily
with our teams and clients. These adages simply
and succinctly remind us of key tenets to create
compelling guest experiences, regardless of whether
it's a theme park, museum, or corporate experience.
*　If Marty had a dollar for every time one of these*
Commandments was used in a meeting, he'd be a
very rich man indeed.

　　　　—Craig Hanna, Chief Creative Officer, Thinkwell

The theme park as a design genre was a new idea
when Disneyland opened in 1955. The films, stories,
and visuals that comprised the park and its attractions
were based in part on tried-and-true elements from
other, older parks; but their intent was totally new:
experiences meant not to separate guests from their

money, but to inform, inspire, and delight. Walt's respect and devotion to Disneyland visitors certainly speaks to what would become the first of Mickey's Ten Commandments—Know your audience. Marty's expansion on the other nine commandments (and ten more later on) is a concise reflection and signpost for the novelty of the Disneyland design—and all parks and resorts beyond. They mark the care and compassion for the guest experience that makes good themed design so special. Marty's credos are broad, firm, but flexible enough to cover museums, aquariums, zoos, and any other place dedicated to transformative, magical experiences. In our unique business, there are few "ancient truths." Marty's simple and eloquent dictums are certainly its gospel. Every good project reflects them, and broken commandments are obvious in poor ones. I think about them every time we start something new, when I walk through a newly opened attraction, when revisiting old ones. Good, simple truths last forever.

—**Garner Holt**, Founder, Garner Holt Productions

Know Your Audience has been critical to the ongoing success of Tokyo Disney Resort (TDR). As the first international Disney park, Tokyo Disneyland began as a very literal copy of its Western counterparts and quickly proved to be successful from opening day. But over time, TDR has evolved as our Japanese guests have evolved. The more our guests embraced TDR as their own, the more we have reflected our Japanese guests in the fabric of the resort. Multiple popcorn flavors, Duffy and Friends, Tanabata (the annual star festival), and even the lottery system to get seats for our shows were all introduced in Tokyo because of the unique tastes and needs of our Japanese guests. While Tokyo Disney Resort has remained authentically Disney, it is also now a reflection of Japan.

Most Imagineers who designed and developed Tokyo Disney Resort will never have the opportunity to visit Tokyo, so I do all I can to teach them about our Japanese guests. When I lived in Japan as the design director for Walt Disney Imagineering Japan, I never took for granted my ability to walk the parks and "wear our guests' shoes" every day. I learned what our guests really care about, what gets them excited, and what causes them stress. By considering the point of view of the guest, I am able to focus and prioritize what is most important.

Communicating with visual literacy is especially important at Tokyo Disney Resort because we have created a Western resort in Japan, a non-Western culture with a non-Western language. When you walk through Tokyo Disneyland, you could easily imagine that you are in the Magic Kingdom at Walt Disney World. All the marquees and major signs are in English. At times the form and design of the graphic sign itself are more important than the wording on the sign. The words "Ice Cream" on a storefront sign are secondary to that sign being the shape of an ice cream cone. Our Japanese guests must be able to walk through the park and its attractions fully understanding the stories we are telling mainly from the design itself. We must consider what every space and detail is conveying to our guests, assuming that they may not be able to read the sign above the door.

Japan is full of apparent contradictions. A couple may have a Christian wedding, be blessed by a Shinto priest, and then have a Buddhist funeral. But to the Japanese, the blend of different cultures is perfectly acceptable and creates a new unique identity. The teams in Japan often are unaware of the contradictions in their proposals because they are so accustomed to such awkward combinations throughout Japan. Strictly speaking, the combination of Japanese culture and our Western Disneyland could itself lead to contradictions. However, I believe that to our guests, Tokyo Disneyland is neither Japan, nor is it purely Disney. It is a special combination bridging both worlds that has itself become a unique identity.

—Daniel Jue, Portfolio Creative Executive, Walt Disney Imagineering

Our Disney destinations operate in an industry that has, quite frankly, exploded with fresh offerings and new experiences, particularly over the last twenty-five years. Yet, Disney still stands apart. Because of this, people often ask us for "the Disney secret," as if there were a single, golden principle that could turn an organization into amazing storytellers and guest-service fanatics. But, just as having only a single great attraction or offering only a single great experience will not earn you a place in the hearts of millions, *paying attention to just one thing won't bring the guests back time and time again. People love Disney because of our unrelenting adherence to a number of time-honored principles: the principles that Marty Sklar has collected and assembled as Mickey's Ten Commandments. This is what has allowed us to assemble a cast in which a passion for memory making and great guest experience is positively contagious. It is what makes Disney . . . Disney.*

*—**George A. Kalogridis**, President, Walt Disney World Resort*

Mickey's (Marty's) Ten Commandments should be bedrock for anyone conceiving and developing guest experiences. Each one of the Ten Commandments is grounded in Marty's many decades of experience at Disney, building and operating some of the most successful theme parks and attractions on earth. I believe the overarching message, and most important commandment, is simple: remember to put yourself in your guests' shoes when designing a guest experience.

At their best, themed entertainment experiences can transport guests to different environments, emotional states, cognitive realities, and, sometimes, just make them laugh. It is all possible when designers embrace Mickey's Ten Commandments.

*—**Monty Lunde**, TEA Founder, President, Technifex*

One of Imagineering's proudest accomplishments is Cars Land, at Disney's California Adventure. I promise, I'm not just saying that because I was the project's executive producer (really!). Cars Land, which opened in 2012, was the first project that told us that guests would embrace an entire land based on one story—the world of Cars, and, more specifically, the tiny little town called Radiator Springs.

I think guests love Cars Land for many reasons— and maybe one of those reasons is because it adheres to all of Mickey's Ten Commandments. Next time you visit the land, take a close look and I think you'll see what I mean.

It's amazing how relevant all of Mickey's Ten Commandments are to this day, but there are two in particular that I think the land really honors. They are commandments we referenced a lot when we were designing the land. They are:

• Tell one story at a time. We did that—you are in the world of Cars. Everything was designed as though it was built by and for cars. There are layers to this storytelling, of course, but they all tell the same story.

• Avoid contradictions—maintain identity. Look around and you'll see flowers with taillights in their centers, neon signs that look like they are straight from Route 66, Ramone's customized hoods on display; there are too many details to mention, but they all work in harmony. Nothing looks out of place.

—**Kathy Mangum,** Retired Forty-Plus Year Imagineer

I first became aware of Marty's Mickey's Ten Commandments before I began working at Disney Imagineering in 1998. It's the hallmark of a statement of deep wisdom that, upon first reading, it immediately makes sense and makes evident all manner of past momentary observations, obscure instincts, deeper truths, and things that should have been obvious . . . but, of course, weren't, until they were so clearly stated and organized.

I can't even guess how many times I have quoted just the first commandment: Know your audience. Much of my work has been abroad: for example in Japan, France, and most recently China. In each case it has been crucial to recognize a priori that the audience will be different in some way by virtue of their history, experience, and the distinct culture that surrounds them (and of which they are an integral part). It is critical to study and understand on an emotional level what the differences are before we can come to the things that we have in common—and of course there are always more things we have in common. That is one of the most life-affirming aspects of our work in this quirky industry.

Marty's words were a reminder to me to see the whole picture, so that the small differences didn't trip up my efforts to reach the audience, even when I thought we'd built around what was seemingly universal. I think that this was a key to our success in creating Shanghai Disneyland, as the team sought from the start to create a Magic Kingdom for mainland China. Our mission was to create an experience that was core Disney, but with language, stories, services—thousands of specific elements—

deftly adjusted for the new audience.

The second group of commandments, about perception, organization, visual icons, visual literacy, prioritizing, and generosity, are fundamental to any creative endeavor that involves storytelling. And every one of them comes back to the guest's point of view. As creators, we are by nature eager to display huge numbers of ideas, and are loath to leave anything behind. Yet it is critical for the enjoyment of our guests that we do the hard work of editing mercilessly, that we create pace and energy, remove confusion, give proper meaning to every element, all the while remaining exuberant and playful. That's the wonderful challenge: create a surprising and joyful experience that is clear and comfortable for the guest to take in, but has greater and greater depth, to engage an increasingly sophisticated audience.

Mickey's Ten Commandments—knowing the people in our audience and creating an experience from their point of view—mean, in essence, respecting our guests. That is quintessential Marty.

—**Luc Mayrand,** Portfolio Creative Executive, Walt Disney Imagineering

Mickey's Ten Commandments were of particular relevance as we designed Shanghai Disneyland. We were tasked with delivering a Disney theme park in mainland China to an audience that had only marginal context at best as to our brand, our product, and our stories. The design teams made several trips to China to better understand everything from demographics to leisure activities, culture, history, family dynamics, storytelling, etc. We went to theme parks, botanical gardens, national parks, museums, historical sites, cultural events; we conducted extensive in-market research; we dined; we shopped. All of which is to say, we took some deep dives into the Chinese market to inform how we tell our stories, how we create environments, how we develop food and beverage programs, how we move guests through public spaces, and how we tap into the emotions and intellect of our Chinese guests.

The individual themes of all of our lands at Shanghai Disney Resort are true and clear: there's no mistaking Treasure Cove for Fantasyland, or Tomorrowland for Mickey Avenue. We had to be deliberately literal and somewhat singular in our place-making to help bring our Chinese guests into our stories—no princesses in Adventure Isle, unless they happen to be part of the ancient Abori people, and none of Pooh's spinning "hunny pots" in the world of the TRON Lightcycles.

At the Shanghai Disney Resort, we have the biggest castle of any theme park; it serves as the park's North Star—you always know where you are by simply looking up . . . way up. At the end of the day, Shanghai Disneyland has strengthened the Disney brand in China through immersive storytelling, compelling environments, and safe and family-friendly guest experiences—all predicated on the team's ability to interpret and apply the lessons of

Mickey's Ten Commandments. The conceits of theme, structure, and identity kept our stories straight and enabled our newly minted Disney guests to feel welcomed and celebrated.

—Jodi McLaughlin, Portfolio Executive Producer, Walt Disney Imagineering

With sixty-one words and a total of 298 characters, Marty created a guiding light for a thousand ships. But Mickey's Ten Commandments reach much farther than Disney's shores. They act like a compass for anyone creating experiences. I have used them with design teams around the globe to create and produce events, museum exhibitions, retail environments, trade shows, and theme park attractions—but not just at Disney. I have worn my guests' shoes while designing Harry Potter: The Exhibition, helped create turn-ons for Twister . . . Ride It Out at Universal Studios Florida, and literally brought a ton of treat to the nationwide film promotions for Pixar's Cars, Cars 2, and Cars 3. It goes without saying that I used them in 2015 to help create the D23 Expo show Disneyland—The Exhibit to celebrate the sixtieth anniversary of the park. Everyone can relate to Mickey's Ten Commandments, because Marty made sure they were relatable and translatable. Marty gave us so much magic during his lifetime, and this list is the sorcerer's spell that never fails!

—Eddie Newquist, Chief Creative Officer, Former Vice President, Universal Studios Creative

Mickey's Ten Commandments were the core message that Marty would deliver to the Bradley University communication, marketing, and public relations students when they journeyed to Los Angeles for their annual January two-week, behind-the-scenes tour of the film and television studios. As a graduate of Bradley University's masters program, I participated in the tour and educational series, lending my expertise in themed entertainment. I always reached out to Marty to deliver an educational session for the students as his good friend John Hench had gifted Bradley University in Peoria, Illinois, with the "John C. Hench Production Arts Studio." (The building was dedicated on October 16, 2007, on the school's campus.) Marty always enthusiastically said yes! He felt that it was important that the knowledge and education he learned over the many years at Disney be passed on in some small way, through Mickey's Ten Commandments, to a new generation of students. Our purpose was to educate and also to inspire the students to look at the industry we loved as a career. It was pure joy to be in the audience on those days to listen to Marty's many stories and watch how the students immediately adopted Mickey's Ten Commandments as their own! They had grown up with Disney and loved everything Disney. You should have seen their smiles when I introduced Marty! The students discovered during Marty's presentations that the Ten Commandments made "total sense" and could be used in every aspect of their careers and life.

As one young graduate student wrote in 2012

after Marty's presentation: "WOW. Thank you, thank you, thank you! Mickey's Ten Commandments was the most important single document I received on this trip! It is a keeper! My life will never be the same! Thank you, Mr. Sklar, for your stories and for inspiring me to DREAM BIGGER!"

—**Roberta Perry,** Vice President,
Edwards Technologies

As an attraction architect, I often found myself exploring a wide range of market opportunities within the TEA industry looking for new challenges. The common denominator for many of my projects—destination properties focused on guest experiences and place making environments. Our work had me working with my dad—Disney Legend Harrison "Buzz" Price—as well as an amazing group of talented industry people on wide ranging projects—theme parks, entertainment districts, resorts, redevelopment, mixed-use projects, themed restaurants, and family entertainment centers. Mickey's Ten Commandments provided a set of core values and objectives that applied to everything we were working on. And then the unexpected happened!

In the mid 1990's, my hospitality experience and "un-churched" persona caught the eye of the church growth community leading to opportunities to speak at conventions and conferences—an audience of believers and faithful. How did this happen? I drew upon what I knew to be true—Mickey's

Ten Commandments—and swapping one set of Commandments for another. It worked! I suddenly found myself master planning mission fields across the country—from California to New Jersey—designing lifestyle settings and "lands" that appealed to the ministry needs of children, families, young adults, and seniors.

What's the takeaway? Mickey's Ten Commandments clearly resonates beyond our TEA industry to an audience and markets that are open to fresh ideas and approaches. Have to thank Marty too! I don't think I would have found my way back from the desert without his guidance.

—**David A. Price,** American Institute of Architects, President & Founder, Price Leisure Group Inc.

My favorite Mickey's Ten Commandments moment happened recently when I was trying to solve a design problem with my core project team in a conference room in Florida. There's a show scene in our new attraction, Mickey's & Minnie's Runaway Railway, in which everyone's favorite couple rises into view hanging tightly on to the strings of a big bunch of balloons. As Mickey's and Minnie's bodies are black—suspended under the balloons while hanging on to each other in this nighttime scene—the two of them looked like one big jumble, because their body lines could not be defined. For the moment to visually read, it was clear Mickey and Minnie needed to be separated. But they still had to be suspended together under the same bunch of balloons. I came *up with the idea that, when the balloons rise into the scene from behind a set piece, the couple would be revealed sitting next to each other on a big hot dog sign broken off from the stand below. Instead of Mickey and Minnie holding on to the strings together, the strings would be tied to either end of the hot dog sign. Before we'd see the perfect pair rise into view, we'd hear Mickey say, "Hot dog! This is gonna work!" Everyone on the team loved this solution to the problem. When we wrapped up our successful meeting and were leaving the conference room, our producer, Charita Carter, noticed a large copy of Mickey's Ten Commandments pinned to the wall next to the door. "Hey, Kev!" she exclaimed. "Marty would be so proud of you." I asked, "Why's that?" Charita pointed to commandment number four. "You created a 'wienie'!"*

—Kevin Rafferty, Executive Creative Director, Walt Disney Imagineering

Common sense is not that common. Perhaps that's why Mickey's Ten Commandments (actually Marty's but he is too modest) are at once a blinding flash of the obvious and a rare peek into a treasure trove of invaluable trade secrets. They are obvious (or should be) in that once you hear them you immediately say, "Yes, of course!" But in the rush to create and design a project these profound insights are so often forgotten that they always feel like a fresh revelation each time they are revisited. That's why I keep my framed copy over my desk so I will look at it and be reminded and re-energized several times each day. I'm not alone. All of the high achievers in my industry know and constantly think about Mickey's Ten Commandments. As a result, this seemingly simple document has been a touchstone supplying magic to our industry's greatest achievements and achievers, not just at Disney but all over the world. Thank you, Marty, for sharing such a valuable gift.

*—**Bob Rogers**, Founder, Chairman and Chief Creative Officer, BRC Imagination Arts*

Knowing your audience is a great lesson in empathy. It's not just about reading a bunch of data from surveys. It is about feeling what they feel, about being emotionally sensitive to their lives and the way they see things. That is a great practice for anyone, whether they are designers or not.

Commandment 3 is one of my favorites. This one concept means so many different things. First of all, you cannot execute a project unless you understand the flow of ideas that makes the project exist. You must be able to articulate what the project is about with a clear flow of ideas. Understanding that flow of ideas allows you to organize the team and the flow of their work, which greatly facilitates their own understanding of the job. That increases the clarity of the design, which ultimately increases the flow of ideas in the mind of the guest and increases their enjoyment of the show.

Our guests may not have visual literacy, but we really need to. Every single element used to tell a visual story can also work against that story unless it is balanced and harmonious. Visual literacy is not just a knack that some people have, it requires study: the study of other great artists, other great projects, the study of the brain and perception, and the study of the world in general. It is precisely because of all of that hard work and study that the story is made clear and easy to understand so that guests can enjoy it. One of the great rules of storytelling is "Show, don't tell." But you can't show anything if you don't understand the visual rules by which things are seen.

No matter how much detail you accumulate . . . it needs to all add up to one thing. This is one of Marty's great lessons. It's often mistaken to mean that you can only tell really simple stories with really simple tools. But that's not the case. The point is that no matter how rich the story is, no matter how much detail it has, no matter how complex it becomes, it is about one great idea.

—**Joe Rohde**, Portfolio Creative Executive, Walt Disney Imagineering

At Imagineering, we look to the Ten Commandments often as a clear reminder of the purpose of our work. First, they remind us that we create experiences not for ourselves but for a wildly diverse audience. Second, we are first and foremost storytellers; our work is most successful when every last detail is informed by a coherent and compelling narrative. Like all great stories, our attractions and places consume our guests and leave them longing for more as they reach the end. Finally, the impact of our work is timeless, and is measured by the lasting joy experienced together by countless millions of people around the globe.

*—**Craig Russell**, Project Integration Executive, Walt Disney Imagineering*

For decades, I've loved sitting on a Main Street bench and watching how the guests react, what works and gets a smile (and what doesn't). To me, Mickey's Ten Commandments were best summarized by Walt himself in a story Marty likes to tell. Walt once explained that the parks were all about "satisfying people's needs"—and he meant their emotional needs. Emotional needs are the reason we get up in the morning; they are our dreams for the future. Meeting those needs means choosing the right themes to fulfill a hidden aspiration, playing just the right song, or directing the smell of candy into the street to trigger a memory. How do you do that without "knowing your audience" or "being in their shoes"? They sense the care, love, nostalgia, or childlike innocence of a reassuring experience when we do that job sincerely and earnestly, not because it promotes a movie or toy. No doubt, Walt knew what he missed from his own childhood, and he knew how to build a family experience that was a "ton of treat" for us to treasure in our own way.

*—**Eddie Sotto**, Former Imagineer, President, SottoStudios*

Marty Sklar, through his ability to codify Mickey's Ten Commandments, has left a most valuable legacy to the creative community on how to initiate and develop world-class themed entertainment projects.

As a member of Disney's Imagineering group leadership in the days of the development of Walt Disney World, Epcot, and Tokyo Disneyland, my colleagues and I pursued these tenets on a daily basis. They were not posted on a wall, but were transferred to our thoughts and actions; originally from Walt Disney directly and passed on and refined throughout the organization where quality and innovation resided without peer.

These commandments have guided my approach to every project that I have initiated, developed and managed during my fifty-seven years in this industry. They are the keys to the delivery of an outstanding themed attraction in an industry occupied by significant creative talent.

Marty has left all of us who inhabit, and those who will enter, this creative community a most valuable, proven roadmap to follow and guide their efforts with Mickey's Ten Commandments.

With sincere appreciation.

—*Frank P. Stanek*, Chairman,
Stanek Global Advisors, LLC

When I first went to Disney, I had never worked on a theme park, a theme park attraction or show. As part of the leadership of a firm led by architect and developer John Portman, I was experienced in planning, designing, and constructing very large complex projects, and that is what theme parks are. Because of my lack of experience in theme parks, I needed to learn as much as I could about them.

Mickey's Ten Commandments were short, clear, and right on target. Once I became aware of them, I began to listen carefully and started to understand the underlying theories that allowed the Imagineers to create Disney-quality theme parks time after time. I slowly began to learn and understand the important principles they followed as they created wonderful attractions, shows, and entire theme parks. Marty referred to what he considered the most important list of dos and don'ts as Mickey's Ten Commandments. However, I know that I learned many more than that number that had varying degrees of importance.

They provided me with the understanding that I needed in order to be most effective in the position in which I was placed. I had very applicable expertise to do my job of managing the development process, but I was completely lacking in the knowledge of the product we were producing. I am confident that I could have learned them through osmosis, but it would have taken a very long time. It was an invaluable gift when I realized that in a very short time I was learning the concepts that the creative people were following, and I did not need to attend lectures or another graduate course or whatever to do so. I *simply had to hang around and listen to Marty and his incredible group of "creatives," and I realized I was learning fast. I could not have done it myself, but by listening to Marty and their discussions, I began to understand why they were doing much of what they were doing. I was soon able to provide effective assistance for their efforts though development and construction and support their success.*

*—**Stanley "Mickey" Steinberg**, Senior Advisor, the Portman Holdings Companies; Former Executive Vice President and Chief Operating Officer, Walt Disney Imagineering*

For the Shanghai Disney Resort project, the commandments were paramount! Working in a foreign culture requires a lot of study. We couldn't assume the audience knew the brands and stories; and at the same time our teams had to learn about the culture, customs, language, trends, etc. We must always remember who we are designing for; it is not for us . . . the designers. This will prevent overdesigning. Be organized and clear with your objectives while designing, and the results will also be organized and clear for your guests. This is called leading the pack to the water hole . . . the water hole where you want them to go . . . then to the next . . . then to the next. The whole story can unfold before a guest's eyes without one word being spoken. Be deliberately detailed, but not fussy! You must create a credible and memorable moment that will last forever, even if it is as simple as a princess's wave to you. Do not confuse the guests. Believe in the power of telling one clear, meaningful story rather than two or more rambling messages. Create rewards at every turn.

*—**Doris Hardoon Woodward,** Executive Creative Producer, Walt Disney Imagineering*

CHAPTER 9

TRAVELLING AND SPREADING "THE WORD"— THE BEST ADVICE I EVER HEARD

More than sixty years ago, as a twenty-two-year-old just beginning my career, I wrote my first words that would appear in print expressing the ideas and inspiration of Walt Disney. It was a daunting task: young Marty, just a year or so after graduating from UCLA with a degree in political science, creating words and phrases to convey the ideas of one of the best-known human beings on the planet.

How to even begin?

Today you would probably Google something about the subject at hand, but in 1956, long before the Internet, I made a pilgrimage to the nearest library. It did not take long to find a book that became my bible, pointing the way to my decade of ghostwriting special material for Walt.

That little book was called *Words to Live By*, a "New Treasury" of essays "selected and interpreted by ninety men and women," according to its title page. First published in

1947, it included advice about goal setting, success, and ways of life by a potpourri of well-known people from many fields, including authors (John Steinbeck and James Michener), military men (General Omar Bradley and Admiral Hyman Rickover), politicians (Herbert Hoover and John Foster Dulles), performers (Maurice Chevalier and Mary Martin), international icons (Albert Schweitzer and Margaret Mead), and, of course, Walt Disney himself.

Walt's words were direct and to the point: "Take a chance!" he implored, and then went on to communicate a message I was to become familiar with over the next decade: "If I'm no longer young in age, I hope I stay young enough in spirit never to fear failure—young enough still to take a chance and march in the parade."

Of course the message itself was an inspiration. But it was much more than the message that sparked my enthusiasm: it was the style, the simplicity, the sincerity of the words that captured my interest. I had met with Walt enough even then to recognize that *this* was the Walt Disney I knew. The writer, long forgotten as ghostwriters usually are, had somehow found a way to make Walt Disney's words jump off the pages of that book. And I had found the voice of Walt Disney, on paper, that I would attempt to emulate for the next decade.

More than that: I took up the quest of *Words to Live By* over the course of my half-century career at The Walt Disney Company. As I have travelled and spoken to audiences around the country (and at sea), I have shared the best of the advice I heard from the many amazing people I've had the good fortune to meet and work with while creating the Disney parks and resorts.

I believe these "Words to Live By" can change your own

life—whether you are in a creative field or simply looking for inspiration to pass to your children. Understanding, using, and sharing these ideas can help you become a better leader, a more vital team player, or a more respected person.

I highlighted some of my favorites in both *Dream It! Do It!* and *One Little Spark!* but there are still more I'd like to share. So in no particular order, here we go:

* * * * * * * * * *

1. **"You've got to bait the hook, but keep the story simple."**
   —Richard Sherman, Songwriter and Lyricist

Few people in the history of Walt Disney entertainment have meant more to the brand than Richard Sherman. Richard and his brother, Robert, created magic in musical story-telling, including the songs and music for *Mary Poppins*, the iconic "it's a small world," and "One Little Spark." Richard continues to write and perform, including the heartwarming tribute to Walt Disney "A Kiss Goodnight," performed at Disneyland with the nightly fireworks show.

"Storytelling is the best way to sell an idea in any sort of situation," Richard wrote. "But remember to keep the story simple. When you get it right, it becomes an implosion of concepts—your idea synthesized in a clean, simple statement of a few words."

2. **"When everything works, it *reassures* people that the world can be OK."**
   —John Hench, Senior Vice President of Design,
   Walt Disney Imagineering

John joined Disney as a sketch artist working on *Fantasia* in 1939 and was still working sixty-five years later when he passed away, in 2004, at age ninety-five. John had been one of Walt Disney's closest associates. His achievements ranged from painting the first official portrait of Mickey Mouse (at Walt's request), to the design of Space Mountain and Epcot's Spaceship Earth. He was my design partner in the creation of Epcot.

John believed passionately in the power of good design to set an example. He argued that guests, having experienced the world inside Disney parks—where you can speak to a stranger in a public place that is clean and organized and where things actually work—would know that "the outside world" can also achieve those standards. In a travelling show we developed with the Canadian Centre for Architecture, John even named the show and the Disney standard "The Architecture of Reassurance."

"We give power to the guests' imagination," John said, "to transcend their everyday routine. Our special notion of form, together with Walt's insistence that our guests should 'feel better because of their experiences in Disney theme parks,' establishes the foundation for the art of the show."

3. "Sometimes all it takes is remembering how to be a child."
> —Pam Fisher, Senior Show Writer (retired), Walt Disney Imagineering

Pam Fisher's contributions to our Disney park shows were typical of so many great talents: she did brilliant work *anonymously*. Among other achievements, Pam developed the script for the classic Indiana Jones Adventure in Disneyland and wrote material for talents as diverse as Morgan Freeman, Dame Judi Dench, and Steve Martin. She also directed the recordings of Presidents George W. Bush and Barack Obama for The Hall of Presidents in Liberty Street at Walt Disney World's Magic Kingdom.

"There is one very large truth about imagination: you don't have to go to art school, wear outrageous outfits, and be flamboyant to have imagination," Pam says. "You just have to be intrigued by words like 'what if' and 'how.' And you have to understand the value of childish things."

4. "Believe in your ideas—no matter how crazy they may seem!"
—Jack Lindquist, first President of Disneyland, first Marketing Chief for Disney Parks & Resorts Worldwide

You met Jack Lindquist in Chapter 2. Jack believed that we were successful in marketing in the early days of Disneyland because "we didn't know what wouldn't work—so we tried anything!" And he proved it again and again—including with the promotion for Disneyland's thirtieth birthday celebration in 1985.

Michael Eisner had just become chairman and CEO of The Walt Disney Company when he called Jack. "Are you the guy that wrote the memo?" Eisner asked Jack Lindquist. "You said we would do twelve million attendance at Disneyland in 1985. That's ridiculous!"

Disneyland's attendance in 1984 was 9.4 million people. "You said if we don't do twelve million in '85, you will resign on January 1, 1986," Eisner continued. "That's a bonus for the company," Lindquist responded. Eisner signed off on "my crazy idea," Jack recalled, "probably because I believed in it wholeheartedly."

The result: sparked by the grandest promotion in Disneyland's history, called "Gift-Giver Extraordinaire," during which every thirtieth, three hundredth, three thousandth, and thirty-thousandth guest received a prize of some sort—including a brand-new General Motors car to every thirty-thousandth visitor—Disneyland's attendance increased 22 percent in 1985, to 12.5 million people!

"To me," Jack Lindquist said, "that's the essential part—believing in your ideas, no matter how crazy they may seem!"

5. **"In brainstorming, there are no bad ideas."**
—Mk Haley, Research Producer,
Disney Research

Mk Haley is one of the most versatile young research talents I watched "grow up" inside and outside of Imagineering and Disney research. A computer animation graduate with a nose for new technology, Mk has excelled in technical and creative roles with virtual reality teams, R & D, and special effects. She has also served as associate executive producer and faculty at the Entertainment Technology Center at Carnegie Mellon University and as Entrepreneur in Residence at Florida State University.

"Brainstorming," Mk says, "is a process that invites creative solutions with riotous, swirling activity, thunderclaps of genius, and sweeping winds of change. Define the challenge.

Collect ideas. Keep going. Brainstorming is a circular process. You do, you learn, you do again from what you learned, and repeat. Now, for the 99 percent perspiration that brings innovation to fruition, follow up with research, implementation, building, testing, and installation."

6. "Build a creative toy chest."
—Maggie Irvine Elliott, Artist,
Community Arts Advocate

Maggie Irvine Elliott survived the burden of being "the boss's daughter" to become senior vice president of creative development administration—in other words, she was the number one administrator of my creative group at Imagineering. Now retired, Maggie began her career riding to Glendale with her father, Imagineering design chief Richard Irvine, to work in the Model Shop. She was so good that, before becoming part of my creative office, she became the head of that Dimensional Design team, as it's now called.

"A creative toy chest stimulates thinking and exercises creative muscles," Maggie shares. "Fill your toy chest with research, knowledge, ideas, and imagination. Shop till you drop! Then pull out all your toys and play the game of creativity. With all the toys in your toy chest, you will discover different aspects of the creative process and multiple ways to express your creativity."

7. "We love the wind!"
—Jackie Cooper, Head Tennis Professional,
La Quinta Resort Tennis Club

I had the good fortune to play in two member–pro tennis tournaments with the late Jackie Cooper. (I was the member; he was the pro.) We won both championships, even beating John Austin and his partner in one of them. (John Austin and his sister, Tracy—twice U.S. Open women's champion—won a Wimbledon mixed-doubles crown.) When we played, the wind was blowing so hard in the California desert that you could hardly keep a hat on your head. As we walked onto the court, I asked my professional partner for instructions, expecting him to say, "Just get the hell out of my way!" But all Jackie Cooper said to me was "We *love* the wind!" In other words, conditions are what they are—on both sides of the net. Life is full of strong breezes; sometimes the wind blows in strange directions. You can't change it, so learn to live with the conditions that come your way. Sometimes you can make even the worst obstacles work for you!

8. "It's kind of fun to do the impossible."
—Walt Disney, Motion Picture and TV Producer,
Creator of Disneyland

On my home office wall, I have a photograph of Walt Disney demonstrating how he wanted an early Audio-Animatronics figure to "perform." Bob Gurr, the great Disney designer who made the original Abraham Lincoln figure work for the 1964–65 New York World's Fair, says the concept Walt was demonstrating *did not work*. "Actually," Gurr said, "it was impossible."

Exactly the point! Having tried—and tried again—to create lifelike "characters" who could "act" sixteen hours a day and provide every guest with a perfect performance (no matter what time of day, without coffee and lunch breaks), Walt kept moving from that early concept. And as a result, today we have not only "Abraham Lincoln," but the singing children of "it's a small world," a dragon in a Parisian castle, Buzz Lightyear, and the iconic swashbuckling buccaneers of Pirates of the Caribbean.

My second note about Walt Disney's advice is about the word "fun." Lest we forget, that's the business we're in, and the expectation of our guests who pay the bills. But as I frequently told my colleagues at Imagineering, it's about them, too. If you're not having fun in the "fun business"—find something else to do!

9. "Does it have to be a light bulb?"
—Kevin Rafferty, Executive Creative Director,
Walt Disney Imagineering

When Disney published the first major hardcover coffee-table book about Imagineering in 1996 (*Walt Disney Imagineering: A Behind the Dreams Look at Making the Magic Real*), the book opened with this by Kevin Rafferty:

Question: *"How many Imagineers does it take to change a light bulb?"*
Answer: *"Does it have to be a light bulb?"*

Kevin's lines simply and directly hit the heart of the spirit of discovery and innovation in our industry. As I later wrote in the section of *One Little Spark!* called "Be Curious":

"When you ask 'why' or 'what if,' you have an inquisitive mind that can lead to new directions and discoveries. Be eager to know and try more: *be curious!*"

* * * * * * * * * *

The Blank Page

In my first two books of Disney and Imagineering stories—*Dream It! Do It!* and *One Little Spark!*—I established a little "tradition."

As the creative leader of Walt Disney Imagineering, I was widely known for my favorite piece of wisdom: "There are two ways to look at a blank page. One way is to see it as 'the most frightening thing in the world'—because you have to make the first mark on that blank page. The second way is to see a blank page as the greatest opportunity in the world—because you get to make that first mark on the blank page!"

For Imagineers, that opportunity is the fascination and fun of our business—the business of creating fun, new experiences, and happy memories for you and your family, our legion of fans and friends around the world.

Now it's your turn to play. Go ahead and make that first mark on this blank sheet of paper. Dream. Create something new. Surprise yourself—it's your chance to be an Imagineer!

The Most Frightening Thing in the World

Illustration by John Horny

MARTY'S LEGACY:
One Little Spark from Him to You!

For most of his career at Disney, Marty Sklar worked behind the scenes—publishing *The Disneyland News*, writing press releases for Disneyland and scripts for Walt Disney, and creating attractions and theme parks. Then, when the curtain was pulled back to reveal some of the magic at WDI, Marty became something of an icon within the themed entertainment industry and especially to Disney fans.

After Marty's passing, messages of appreciation, both public and private, reinforced one important truth: the Marty his family knew was the same Marty his colleagues and fans knew. Professionally and personally, he was encouraging, quick-witted, creative, dedicated, and kind.

Having worked closely with Walt Disney, especially in putting Walt's vision into words, Marty was considered an important keeper of the flame. Disney chairman and CEO

Bob Iger, in the corporate press release reporting Marty's death, put it this way:

Everything about Marty was legendary—his achievements, his spirit, his career. He embodied the very best of Disney, from his bold originality to his joyful optimism and relentless drive for excellence. He was also a powerful connection to Walt himself. No one was more passionate about Disney than Marty and we'll miss his enthusiasm, his grace, and his indomitable spirit.

Marty's connection to Walt and his imprint on Imagineering were described by Bob Weis, president of Walt Disney Imagineering:

Marty was one of Walt's most trusted advisors and helped turn his most ambitious dreams into reality. For us, it's hard to imagine a world without Marty, because Marty is synonymous with Imagineering. His influence can be seen around the world, in every Disney park, and in the creative and imaginative work of almost every professional in the themed entertainment industry.

Frank P. Stanek, Marty's longtime colleague and friend, shared his thoughts:

I received the sad news of Marty's passing yesterday afternoon while parked under a hundred-year-old walnut tree in the small farming town of Spreckels here in Monterey's wine country. As I reflected upon the news, I thought of the fifty-five years that I have known Marty. He was a colleague and a friend, and, like the walnut tree that shaded me, he covered the creative community with wisdom and guidance over his many years of life. Like the walnut tree, which scatters leaves and fruit in the fall, Marty sprinkled his wisdom, insights, guidance, and affection among us all. He was the "Imagine" in "Imagineering," the defender of "quality wins out," the communicator of concepts emanating from "blue sky" meetings, the beacon of principle and clear direction, a mentor to all, and an educator both in passion and for a legion of future creators who will benefit from his generosity.

A personal message from George Kalogridis, president of Walt Disney World Resort, speaking on behalf of the entire cast in Florida, summed up their view of Marty's importance to the resort:

The Florida sunshine shone a little less brilliantly this morning, as we woke up to learn that Marty had moved on.

We come to work every day in a place that he imagined into existence. Our opening day cast members recall that Marty was our True North during construction, the person who made certain that everything we created and did was true to the heart of the Disney brand. When we opened the park to guests for the very first time, Marty was there, as he was for every park opening, right up through Shanghai. . . .

Even among the youngest of our number, there was excitement and more than a bit of awe every time we learned that Marty was on property. Ours is a fairly staid group—we regularly see A-list celebrities in our parks, and greet them no differently than we would a family from Middle America. But when Marty would visit, we lost all pretense of reserve; our newer cast members would stand in line for hours for the opportunity to meet him or shake his hand. Marty, gentleman that he was, would be gracious with each young person, listening attentively regardless of the temperature or the hour, and offering encouragement and advice to every single one.

Marty's passion for quality and excellence extended beyond Imagineering and throughout the business of themed entertainment. His work with the Themed Entertainment Association (TEA) and its Thea selection committee will continue to resonate.

I am one of the thousands whose life has been touched and enriched by the gentle, generous, genius man that was our Marty. . . . I'm probably not alone in thinking that the Themed Entertainment Association enjoys its very existence to the support of Disney, championed by Marty. His devotion to recognizing and developing talent permeates all of Disney's outreach programs and transforms life experiences through the Ryman Arts Foundation. . . . His loss leaves a gigantic crater in our industry and in the hearts of all of us who felt incredibly lucky to be able to call him a friend and a colleague.

—Patricia MacKay, longtime member of the TEA's Thea Awards Nominating Committee

If Walt Disney was the visionary creator of what we call themed entertainment today, Marty represents the soul of our community. Marty has influenced generations of creators and designers at Disney, within TEA and through Ryman Arts. It's hard to imagine anyone in our industry having more impact on so many. I'm one of scores of people who would wholeheartedly claim to be a "Marty Mentee." There was no one more eloquent and dedicated to keeping Walt's visions and dreams alive, or more supportive of individuals and organizations focused on elevating the entire themed entertainment community.

—Monty Lunde, President, Technifex

Of all the icons in the themed entertainment industry, Marty is arguably the greatest of all—measured by the impact his career at Imagineering has had on our industry and all those he touched along the way. I don't think the TEA had a more vocal and active champion. . . . As for me, I was in awe of his insight, wisdom, focus, and sincerity in every meeting we held at the TEA. Indeed, there were several very strong egos in those meetings, but when Marty spoke, everyone listened. The sheer respect for him was unmistakable—but he had a way of wielding the power of that wisdom in the most respectful and supportive ways. He was an absolute gentleman who honored everyone's point of view and was always able to articulate his insights with wit and simplicity no matter the subject.

—Larry Wyatt,
Principal, Wyatt Design Group

Marty made Imagineers. He had a way of intuiting that people had something more to give, and of finding opportunities for them to do that. This was something much more subtle than just recognition of talent. It was a human thing, a recognition of something inside a person that could be cultivated into the total combination of features it takes to be an Imagineer. That takes a lot of empathy, a lot of attention, a lot of patience, and a lot of faith. Marty had all of these, as I know very well, because they were tested constantly by myself, and others, whom he grew into the leaders we are today. In his passing, we lose not just a single person, but an entire fertile epicenter for the beginning of many other persons. It's comforting to know that his legacy lives on through the lives and careers of so many whom he created. But it is equally true that we are now another echo further away from the golden age of Walt Disney himself, and that some of that magic, so clearly infused in Marty, passes now from us and into the stars.

—Joe Rohde, Portfolio Creative Executive,
Walt Disney Imagineering

Marty Sklar was a pivotal mentor to so many. Through his books and speeches, he has touched almost everyone in our industry. Those Marty personally mentored or encouraged (even briefly!) are today doing a better job of leading, mentoring, and encouraging others because of him. The things he taught remain timeless insights into our art and craft. And by the way he personally conducted himself, Marty set a high standard of integrity and generosity. If those of us in this business today are any good at what we do, it is only because we are standing on the shoulders of giants. Marty was one of those giants. And a particularly big one at that.

—Bob Rogers, BRC Imagination Arts

Marty often said that Walt Disney's death affected him more profoundly than the death of his own father, because he had learned to think and write in Walt's voice. For many Imagineers, too, Marty fulfilled the role of a father:

Marty's greatest attribute was not all of his many accomplishments, but his remarkable humanity. He quietly demonstrated so many lessons . . . his never-ending concern for education, for mentoring young people, and finding that perfect moment when one encouraging comment or piece of advice could become the spark that propelled a young person's career or character.

Marty had the rare ability to treat everyone as a special individual . . . no doubt because he believed that to be so. It feels presumptuous to say it, but I

feel like Marty was a kind of second father to me, and I have spoken to literally dozens over the past few days who feel the same way. He was a role model and an exemplar of living a meaningful life that I will carry with me and do my best to emulate.
—Phil Hettema, Founder, The Hettema Group

Marty was to me something like a professional "oncle d'Amérique," the one you don't meet often but you know you can count on him, the one you deeply admire and you feel is making you better, the one you like to know is existing. . . . And a smile which will never pass.
—Yves Pepin, Producer and Creative Director of large-scale multimedia events worldwide

No one has had more influence on Imagineers and Disney parks since Walt Disney himself. Marty, like Walt, was an American original, a powerhouse of creativity, a courageous pioneer, a game-changer, a life-changer, a dreamer, and a doer. And like Walt, he was loved by all. We could not have asked for a better boss, mentor, teacher, advocate, and dear and cherished friend.

But to me he was more than that. He was family. He "raised" me in my career and I feel so blessed I was there during Marty's remarkable, prolific era when he was the heart and soul of Walt Disney Imagineering. I could not be more proud that I was one of his "kids."
—Kevin Rafferty, Executive Creative Director, Walt Disney Imagineering

Marty's "parenting" style with his "kids" was encouraging and supporting, but he maintained control over the direction of the projects. It was one of the secrets to his success working with creative people in a wide array of disciplines.

I worked with Marty and his Imagineers nearly continuously as a graphics consultant since 1974. We played at least some role in ten Disney theme parks and recently saw two nice assignments fulfilled in Shanghai. Until a few years ago, I knew him only as one tough and demanding client. He had a finger on the pulse of everything around him, and no detail was too small for his often-acerbic red pen. You went into Marty meetings prepared or else.

But then around 2006 I joined him on the board of his beloved Ryman Arts and got to know the real, or whole, Marty. The patient, inspiring, almost fatherly guy who worked tirelessly to shape Ryman Arts into the nationally respected arts teaching organization. Watching him lead a board meeting was inspiring and a great learning experience in itself. Marty was still a prolific personal note writer, inscribing each of hundreds of invitations to Ryman Arts events each year, yes, in red marker. He was a master fund-raiser, he said, because he believed so much in the cause.

In 2014, I took over for Marty as board president of Ryman Arts—talk about gigantic shoes to fill!—and that's when I really found out what he had done so beautifully for twenty-five years. Let me tell you, it ain't easy being Marty.

—Wayne Hunt, Founding Principal, Hunt Design

When you were in his presence, he was there with you. He always listened well, was never too hurried or busy to make time for me, and was genuinely interested in what I had to say. He listened more than he talked. He asked questions more than he gave directions; he gave the creatives room to solve seemingly impossible puzzles on our own, by simply nudging us in the right direction and letting us work out the impossible. Marty was a great editor and writer, with a wonderful sense of humor.

—Zofia Kostyrko-Edwards, Artist. Former Imagineer, Conceptual Designer and Art Director Principal, deZign sKape LLC

He embodied Disney, leadership, vision, and inspiration—always pushing us to do more, to believe more, to tackle the impossible. He taught us many things about design and what Disney's theme park experiences should be; he became the voice inside my head. Yes, many buck slips of "Hang in there," "Keep going," "We'll figure this out," and then "Good job." That kind of personal connection made him more than a mentor, inspirational figure: he was like a second dad, always pushing us to be the best we could be— holding Imagineers to an almost impossible standard. Frustrating at times, because his words carried such weight. He didn't just ask the question "What would Walt do?" He became "what Walt would have done."

—Susan Bonds, CEO and Founder, 42 Entertainment

I don't think there's a single person on our TEA committee whose life and career wasn't shaped in some way by Marty Sklar. He was a "Dad" to our entire industry. . . . Over the years, Marty encouraged us all, challenged us, praised us, and let us know when we were right—or wrong. And no matter how much we grew, we never stopped wanting to impress him.
—Adam J. Bezark, President/Creative Director, The Bezark Company, Inc.

Marty was not one of those leaders who thought he had all the answers. On the contrary, he was a leader who helped us all find the pieces to the never-ending array of creative puzzles that we faced.
—Kym Murphy, Retired Imagineering Executive

Though I only knew him for a brief period of time, I will not soon forget Marty Sklar. His insight, his wisdom, his dry sense of humor will live on in my memory. I will also take away from the experience [of collaborating on the travelling exhibition Behind the Magic: 50 Years of Disneyland] an important lesson that I can apply to my work and my life every day: the skillful way in which he could somehow, simultaneously, both encourage wild creativity and make sure that everyone aligned with a larger vision. It sounds easy. But it's not. That to me was the mark of true genius.
—Donna Braden, Curator of Public Life, Henry Ford Museum

Guiding, encouraging, mentoring—these actions can all be attributed to Marty's character, personal integrity, *mensch-iness*, as many remarked.

The Yiddish word mensch communicates a lot of what Marty always represented for me. He was someone who took real responsibility, but he did it with contagious humor and great warmth. Marty had a keen intelligence about other people, what made them tick and how they might contribute to the group. It made him an outstanding leader at Disney and as chair of the Ryman Arts board. This ability to foster the group was natural to Marty—it was part of his nature. I know I will often ask myself, "What would Marty do?" Marty's friendship and example will be a gift that continues in my and many other peoples' lives.
  —Ruth Weisberg, Professor,
  USC Roski School of Art and Design

Marty was nothing short of a force of nature. A creative genius, whose sharp mind was matched by his warm heart. A brilliant and insightful thinker, whose intellect was matched by his menschiness. On top of all of that, he managed to combine a lifetime of truly legendary and world-class experiences and achievements with being one of the most down-to-earth people I've ever met.
  —Dan Adler, former Vice President,
  Creative Development, Walt Disney Imagineering

He was so generous to UCLA in so many ways and

*always encouraging of new ideas. He was full of
intellectual energy and always ready to help with his
ideas and wisdom, which came from the successful
career he had and from his positive attitude, always
looking for the good that could come out of all kinds
of situations, including the challenging ones. He was
a model for me of how to be a mensch. He was loved
by everyone who met him at UCLA, and I know that
so many people will miss him.*

—Alessandro Duranti,
Distinguished Professor of Anthropology, UCLA

*Mentor, leader, and father figure, Marty's influence
throughout this industry is broader and deeper than
anyone will ever know. He was the true Sorcerer's
Apprentice, not just curating and teaching Walt's
principles, but expanding and refreshing them,
forever demonstrating how these timeless truths
remained connected, insightful, and powerful in a
constantly changing world. And he was one of the
nicest, kindest people I ever met.*

—Bob Rogers, BRC Imagination Arts

So many people have told us that Marty personally
changed their lives. More than one person told us that it
was Marty who was responsible for them being married!
More often, we heard that Marty's impact began professionally and became personal—he gave them their start
at Imagineering, or he encouraged them to take a chance
on something new at Imagineering, or he supported their
search for new opportunities outside the company.

Marty was a huge, positive influence in my life (as with so many others!), a true mentor and a wonderful friend! He had a profound impact on my life; it's no exaggeration to say that most of what I've accomplished in my thirty-eight-year career would not have happened (or been possible) without his belief in me, mentorship, and support!
—Kurt Haunfelner, Principal,
KEH Creative Consulting LLC

Marty was a teacher, a mentor, a motivator, and a role model for me for over forty years. He played a critical role in guiding my career and in shaping my life, and I will miss him immeasurably. I've never known anyone who worked with more determination, intellectual brilliance, focus, discipline, passion, and creativity than Marty.
—Barry Braverman, Former Imagineering Executive

Emotional evidence of Marty's personal connection and impact arrived in his e-mail inbox the day after his passing:

Dear Marty,

I'm heartbroken to lose you and our cherished friendship of over thirty-six years. I couldn't have lived my adult life and have my childhood dreams come true as I have done without your help, guidance and without you opening some really big doors for me. You gave me the once-in-a-lifetime chance to prove myself worthy enough to wear an Imagineering name tag and to join the ranks of my Disney Imagineering heroes.

It rips me apart knowing that we will never again be able to see each other and have another wonderful lunch together; that I won't be able to share my life with you, and you share your life with me, any further; that you won't be able to answer my e-mails with funny replies or great stories anymore.

Thank you again for everything! You will always be in my heart, and I will be forever grateful for your mentoring, caring friendship, and love.

Love,

Mouse Silverstein

* * * * * * * * * *

As time marched on after Marty's passing, he was honored in a number of creative and touching ways. Gwendolyn Rogers of The Cake Bake Shop in Indianapolis created Marty Sklar's Chocolate Orange Cake. It's beautiful and delicious! The folks at Hong Kong Disneyland Installed Marty's General Store, where guests can pick up their Disney PhotoPass pictures, purchase pins (he loved those pins!), and more.

We were asked to "represent" at events Marty surely would have attended. These included the retirement party for Diane Scoglio (who had always found just the right illustrative photo at the Imagineering Research Center for Marty's books and speaking engagements) and another recently for Sally Judd, who over her forty-four years with the company had held many jobs at Imagineering, not least of which was executive assistant to Marty.

We attended a reunion at Imagineering celebrating the

thirty-fifth anniversary of the openings of Tokyo Disneyland and EPCOT Center—and the hard work of the people who helped create those parks. There were screenings of a Marty memorial video, compiled beautifully by Mike Iwerks, and event organizer Debbie DelMar provided three storyboards for attendees to post their red pen buck slips, photos, and other mementos in memory of Marty. Debbie generously collected the items on the "Marty Wall" and presented them to us in an album that provides "tons of fun"!

We were also thrilled to be invited to Imagineering on January 26, 2018, for the very first Marty Sklar Legacy Award ceremony. After viewing the entries and chatting with the ImagiNations finalists, we remained on hand as the inaugural award was presented to Dex Tanksley for his dedication to the ImagiNations program, which had been not only a favorite and important program of Marty's but also Dex's entry to Imagineering. No one could have been more deserving than Dex!

At UCLA, Marty's contributions to his alma mater were recognized with the establishment of the Marty Sklar My Last Lecture Award, which is given by the school's alumni association to a professor selected by students as their favorite. In May 2018, Imagineer and UCLA alumnus Dave Crawford spoke warmly of Marty and introduced professor Bill Simon, who gave an inspiring "last lecture" before the assembled students and alumni.

In recognition of Marty and Leah's tireless efforts in building Ryman Arts into the successful nonprofit arts education program that it is, the Marty and Leah Sklar Creative Visionary Award was created. At an event that became the most successful fund-raiser to date for Ryman Arts, Leah spoke of her and Marty's commitment to the program, and Bob Weis presented the inaugural award to Kevin Feige, president of Marvel Studios and a true believer in the value of the Ryman Arts program.

Bob Weis graciously invited us to be his guests at the twenty-fourth annual TEA Thea Awards ceremony. At the event, held at the Disneyland Hotel, Phil Hettema justly received the Buzz Price Thea Award for a Lifetime of Distinguished Achievements. The evening's theme was "Celebrate the Creative Spark!" and the program book contained a passage called "Remembering the 'Dad' of an Industry," written by Adam Bezark, chair of the TEA Thea Awards Committee, as well as testimonials from members of the Thea Awards Committee. Adam noted, "For his visionary leadership, his tireless mentorship, and his eternal friendship, the Thea Awards Nominating Committee is honored to dedicate this year's slate of Thea Awards to our friend, our mentor, our colleague, and our 'Dad' . . . Marty Sklar," and quoted Bob Weis:

> Marty's approach to creative challenges, his relentless pursuit of excellence, and his fearless embrace of bold ideas will be influencing artists and innovators generations from now. But—most important—Marty was Marty. He loved all of us, knew us all by name, and enjoyed the process of collaboration and creativity. And as important as he felt it all was, he never took it so seriously that we couldn't have a good time while making the impossible possible.

Bob Rogers provided the visual evidence of Marty's

influence and legacy when he gave this interactive speech in tribute:

Last year we said good-bye to a creative leader, a teacher, a mentor, and a true friend: Marty Sklar.

Tonight, we have with us Marty's wife, Leah, and their daughter, Leslie. Welcome.

It was in 1955, just across the street from where you are all sitting now, Marty Sklar began what became not just over a half century of work. It was a calling.

***Within** Disney he played a creative leadership or mentoring role in the creation of the Disney theme parks and a creative leadership or mentoring role in the creation of the Imagineers.*

*But **outside** Disney he directly or indirectly played a creative or mentoring role **in the creation of . . .** all of **us!***

*After all, it was for **US**, he wrote and lectured, becoming our Sorcerer's Apprentice, channeling, documenting, codifying, **and sharing** wisdom from Walt and from the incredible talent surrounding him.*

Marty was an early advocate for the Thea Awards, championing great work, not just Disney's but deserving achievements everywhere.

With Leah and others, he co-founded Ryman Arts, providing college-level art instruction to high school age artists of exceptional talent. And with Leah he served countless hours, raising money so its students never paid a penny for anything, not even art supplies.

Marty was a giver. He was a mentor to me. But not just to me. What about you?

Who in this room tonight received encouragement, or wisdom, or mentoring from Marty directly or indirectly? If you did, stand up now and remain standing.

*Who else? Who here tonight gained insight from something Marty wrote, maybe **Mickey's Ten Commandments** or one of Marty's books or lectures or panels? If so, join us! Stand up now and remain standing.*

*If you benefitted from a program, class, project, opportunity, or tradition that Marty helped create or nurture—**such as the Thea Awards!**—stand up and remain standing.*

Wow. Look around.

You *. . . are Marty's legacy.*

You *are Marty's legacy.*

*Marty's gift to all of us wasn't in telling us what to create or how to create it. His gift was helping us find and nurture that **one little spark of imagination** within ourselves—that one little spark of imagination that now lives within all of you. That's why, whenever I hear that Sherman brothers' song I will always think of Marty, and smile.*

By the end of Bob Rogers's speech, the entire room was standing and applauding Marty and his legacy as the Aftershock Men's Chorus appeared onstage to lead the hall in singing one of Marty's favorite songs by Richard and Robert Sherman, "One Little Spark":

One Little Spark
Of inspiration
Is at the heart
Of all creation
Right at the start of everything that's new
One little spark
Lights up for you

Imagination
Imagination
A dream can be a dream come true
With just that spark
In me and you!

One bright idea
One right connection
Can give our lives
A new direction
So many times we're stumbling in the dark
And then "Eureka!"
That little spark!

Imagination
Imagination
A dream can be a dream come true
With just that spark
In me and you!

One Little Spark
One flight of fancy
Shines up the dark

So that we can see
When things look grim and nothing's going right
One little spark
Clicks on the light!

Imagination
Imagination
A dream can be a dream come true
With just that spark
In me and you

Two tiny wings
Eyes big and yellow
Horns of a steer
But a lovable fellow
From head to tail he's a royal purple pigment
And then, "Voilà!"
You've got a Figment

Imagination
Imagination
A Dream can be a dream come true
With just that spark
In me and you!

We couldn't think of a more fitting way to remember Marty. Keep dreaming! Keep doing! Keep creating!

—Leslie A. Sklar
For the Marty Sklar Family

ACKNOWLEDGMENTS

Travels with Figment: On the Road in Search of Disney Dreams is very much Marty Sklar's book. But it's also true that it wouldn't have arrived without the considerable efforts of a number of determined individuals.

Wendy Lefkon, Marty's "favorite Disney Editions editor"— and ours as well!—kept the project alive with her creative combination of patience and persistence. Having worked with Marty on numerous Imagineering books and on his two personal books, Wendy knew just how to approach the nearly-completed book after Marty's passing. We are ever grateful for her guidance and compassion.

Who better to write a preface to Marty's book than the current president of Walt Disney Imagineering? We treasure Bob Weis' heartfelt piece, which honors his late predecessor while building on his legacy.

Richard Curtis, Marty's literary agent, wisely stayed the

course with occasional prompts, allowing us time to gather our courage to complete the book.

If you think *Travels with Figment* looks good, so do we! Thanks to Winnie Ho for creating a beautiful cover design that captures the fun vibe of a Marty Sklar book. Chris Runco's take on Marty presenting Mickey's Ten Commandments (to a rapt audience, one presumes) carries the humor to the back cover. When it came time to select photos for inclusion in this book, David Stern at the Walt Disney Imagineering Archives and Collections gamely searched for the unsearchable—and found them! And what's a book called *Travels with Figment* without a Figment? Thanks to Ethan Reed for giving Marty an adorable companion for his travels.

To all of the Imagineers, colleagues, friends, and family who kept reminding us that they wanted to see "Marty's last book" in print: We felt your encouragement and support, and it kept us going when thoughts of "what did Marty want" might have held us back.

We are deeply honored to have been granted permission to publicly share the tributes and condolences that were privately shared with us. If you didn't fully comprehend Marty's legacy before, these moving and very personal memories and reflections on his influence will deepen your understanding and appreciation of the man and his career.

Lastly, no Marty Sklar book could ever be completed without Leah Sklar there every step of the way. Her strength, wisdom, sharp-eyed proofreading, and loving resolve were the essential ingredients that brought this book to you.